The Tattooed Jesus

TITLES FROM GENERATIONS WITH VISION

Family Bible Study Guides
Genesis: A Family Bible Study Guide
Psalms I: A Family Bible Study Guide
Psalms II: A Family Bible Study Guide
Psalms III/IV: A Family Bible Study Guide
Psalms V, Part I: A Family Bible Study Guide
Proverbs I: A Family Bible Study Guide
Proverbs II: A Family Bible Study Guide
Proverbs III: A Family Bible Study Guide
Matthew: A Family Bible Study Guide

Keep The Faith Series
Volume 1: On Education
Volume 2: On Family & Sexuality

Christian Curriculum Project
Great Christian Classics: Four Essential Works of the Faith
Great Christian Classics: Five Remarkable Narratives of the Faith
What Does the Bible Say About That?
Proverbs: A Companion Lesson Book for Children

Apostate: The Men who Destroyed the Christian West
The Second Mayflower
Upgrade: 10 Secrets to the Best Education for Your Child

Audio/Media Resources
Vision for Generations (MP3)
Vision for Generations (CD)
Vision for Generations (DVD)
Family Economics & Discipleship (MP3)
Family Economics & Discipleship (DVD)

The Tattooed Jesus

What Would the Real Jesus Do with Pop Culture?

Kevin Swanson

GENERATIONS WITH VISION
www.generationswithvision.com

ISBN: 978-0-9910439-6-5

Production Management: Joshua Schwisow
Cover Design & Typography: Winslow Robbins
Interior Layout & Design: Winslow Robbins

Published by
Generations with Vision
10461 South Parker Road
Parker, Colorado 80134
www.generationswithvision.com

For more information on this and
other titles from Generations with Vision,
visit www.generationswithvision.com or call 1-888-839-6132.

Contents

Preface

Christian conservatives are finally admitting that they have lost the political war in this country. They are on the "losing side of the cultural war."[1] There is no point in fighting the political wars, if they fail to engage the cultural wars. And, there is no use fighting the cultural wars, if they have already lost the faith and the substance of a Christian worldview. Why fight the political battles when the millennial generation is far more likely to accept homosexual marriage, socialism, and evolution?[2]

I understand the reticence to fight these battles. The cultural battles are more controversial, more difficult, more personal and more fundamental than the political battles. They are more likely to offend our own children and our friends. They force us to confront larger problems and more fundamental problems that involve the social, educational, and cultural institutions that we have grown up with. The cultural icons are impregnable. Conservative Republicans are more committed to Disney than they are to the homosexual agenda. Yet what these conservatives refuse to accept is that Disney is more committed to the homosexual agenda than they are to the Democratic Party.[3]

Perhaps more is at stake here. In the cultural wars, we fight for our own children, our families, and what remains of the church of Christ. Political forces take our money, but they cannot as easily take our souls. They readily permit evil men to do more evil, but they cannot as easily coerce a righteous man to evil. The same cannot be said for the cultural forces. In the political war, the enemy presents itself in true colors. It is much harder to discern the enemy in the cultural war.

Dare I say it? The cultural war tests the true commitment of the human heart. Politics is the business of hypocrisy. Conservatives grudgingly admit to it, and liberals build monuments to their hypocrisy. However, the cultural war eschews hypocrisy from the outset. The battle requires men and women who are honestly and consistently committed to truth and righteousness, or there is no war.

The cultural war is evident all around us, every day. The political war engages mainly during the fall months every year or so. The cultural antithesis is so manifestly accessible that you could spit out the window and hit some Goliath or another.

It's about time for a book about culture—a book that engages the cultural war where the battle is joined with the greatest intensity and relevance. What Christians need is a delineation of the battle lines in Hollywood and Nashville. They need to know what questions to ask, how worldviews are represented in culture, how to recognize trends, and how to discern between that which is good and that which is evil. Where discerning Christians avoid syncretism in worldview and culture, there remains hope that Christian faith and life will still thrive during the decline and fall of the Western world.

Introduction

When Miley Cyrus rode a wrecking ball in the buff for a recent music video, it didn't take a PhD in Cultural Studies to interpret the message. Western culture is committing suicide. The last few living culture critics, including feminist writer Camille Paglia, are complaining of Pop culture's artlessness, sexlessness, and self-destructiveness. Paglia suggests that Lady Gaga, the other major popular star of the day, may be the "exhausted end of the sexual revolution."[1] Decadence is now crossing over into self-immolation, and Pop stars like Miley Cyrus and Lady Gaga are taking billions of people with them. A society cannot remain fixated on decadence forever. Eventually, it must advance to the next logical step—suicide—unless, of course, God has mercy.

The avant garde was trying to tell us that it was over when Andy Warhol painted the Soup Can and somebody paid $15 million for it.[2] But it took another fifty years for the rest of the masses to get the message. The "Pop culture machine" has helped the process immensely.

Back in the 20th century, T.S. Elliot predicted the end of culture with the end of Christian culture:

> "It is in Christianity that our arts have developed; it is in Christianity that the laws of Europe—until recently—have been rooted. It is against a background of Christianity that all of our thought has significance. An individual European may not believe that the Christian faith is true, and yet what he

says, and makes, and does will all spring out of his heritage of Christian culture and depend upon that culture for its meaning... I do not believe that culture of Europe could survive the complete disappearance of the Christian faith. And I am convinced of that, not merely because I am a Christian myself, but as a student of social biology. If Christianity goes, the whole culture goes. Then you must start painfully again, and you cannot put on a new culture ready made. You must wait for the grass to grow to feed the sheep to give the wool out of which your new coat will be made. You must pass through many centuries of barbarism. We should not live to see the new culture, nor would our great-great-great-grandchildren: and if we did, not one of us would be happy in it."[3]

ISLANDS

As the fires burn the last remains of Western civilization to the ground, one wonders if there will be anything left to salvage. T.S. Elliot seemed to think that only barbarism would survive. However, I wonder...what if there were a few Christians left? What if there were Christians who created the occasional oasis of culture in the wasteland of "empty cisterns and exhausted wells?" What if there were faith, hope, and love somewhere in the world? Then perhaps our children, grandchildren, and great grandchildren would thrive in it.

This shift began with the great Christian apostasy. There was first a reversal in the mind of Western man regarding the nature of reality, truth, and ethics. It was a change in worldview, wherein doubt prevailed and truth faded. There was not the faintest possibility of an absolute in the mind of post-modern man. He had lost contact with reality, and he could no longer identify a transcendent purpose for life. A hundred years later, the culture changed to better fit the zeitgeist: the predominant worldview of the age.

I am hopeful, because I believe that there are islands of community, culture, and freedom already forming. Wherever islands of a Christian social order reappear, a distinctly Christian culture may also develop. When the cultural Titanic begins to sink, there are always "life-raft manufacturing centers." Some may prefer to work the "duct-tape repair units" in the engine room of the ship. At some point, however, the focus must shift to the life rafts. That is what is happening now.

There is still something to salvage. For one thing, Western culture still retains some remnants of 2000 years of Christian heritage. A headlining Broadway and Las Vegas show in the 2010's celebrates fornication, and employs the provocative title *Rock of Ages*. Sure, 99.8% of the attendees will have forgotten the old hymn written by Augustus Toplady. To this day, the walls of these humanist empires yet bear the faint marks of a Christian heritage. There is always something that remains, something to strengthen (Rev. 3:2). Empires will come and go, but the empire of the Son continues. Here we find the raw materials upon which to rebuild Christian culture. When everything appears to be rotting and dying around us, something still lives. There will always be a remnant to plant the gardens in the ashes of what used to be a Christian civilization. This was the conclusion of another book I wrote, called *Apostate*.[4]

WHY I WROTE THIS BOOK

I wrote this book because I wanted to read a book that discussed culture, confronted culture, and saved something of Christian culture. As a young man in my 20s, I was fairly well immersed in popular culture through secular radio and film. I worked as a disc jockey on a number of radio stations, covering Adult Contemporary, Rock, Country, Oldies, and Contemporary Christian genres.

Though the influence of popular culture, Country music, and Hollywood films is ubiquitously shot through our society, there has been too little interaction and confrontation with it on the part of Christians. I couldn't find a single book in Christian book stores that dealt with the broader questions addressing artistic media. So, it was with some trepidation I embarked on this study. Cultures are not easily interpreted or analyzed. To say that all popular culture is of the devil is a false statement and produces a weak position. We have had enough of sham religion from those who have attempted to address this cultural milieu without cogent biblically-based ethical arguments. To consign all of Western culture to the devil also ignores the 2000-year reign of Jesus Christ.

However, to *not* interact with modern culture is even more dangerous. The cosmic battle of worldviews takes place right here. The principalities and powers, the rulers of the darkness of this world with which we wrestle (Eph. 6:12), are the trillion dollar institutions and the cultural icons in the West. As I will point out in this book, it was critical for the present apostasy that The Beatles kicked off their career in the choir of their local Anglican parish church. It was critical that Miley Cyrus was baptized into the Southern Baptist church in 2006, and that Katy Perry was raised by her Christian pastor father and mother in Santa Barbara, California. Popular culture reflects the apostasy, because that is the zeitgeist of the Western world.

There is much material that address a Christian worldview, as contrasted with other prevalent worldviews of the day. But these are hardly useful to the masses, unless they connect the dots between the worldview and the cultural incarnations. Most people do not sit and study worldviews all day, but they will go to the movies and listen to Top 40 radio stations. Unless Christian families can properly see the connections between cultures and the worldviews they reflect, many more will be "spoiled by philosophies and vain deceit after the traditions of men." (Col. 2:5). My objective is to work the salvage operation, as we protect and preserve the Christian faith in the West.

1: Following the Trajectory

From Patty Page to Lady Gaga

As I walked into the Christian Booksellers Association convention some eight years ago, I was immediately greeted at the entrance by a vendor sporting the trademark, "Good Newz Tattoos." This scene gave me pause to think. In the "cool" Jesus vernacular of the day, I ask the simple question, "WWJT?" What would Jesus tattoo? Would He tattoo Leviticus 19:28 on his left thigh, for example? Would He wear one earring or two? Would He wear a "No Fear" t-shirt? Would He wear skinny jeans? Would He endorse *Batman Begins*? Would He play fantasy football? Would He buy a Dallas Cowboys season pass? What would Jesus do?

These do seem to be important questions, although they may make us a little uncomfortable. Do any of these musings smack of blasphemy, or are they reasonable considerations? Sincere Christians have arrived at widely differing conclusions concerning these matters, as evidenced in the diversity of cultural expressions found in Western Christianity today. Indeed, many professing Christians do believe that Jesus would tattoo Leviticus 19:28 on his left thigh, pierce his head with metal studs, and cremate His family members upon their death. Other professing Christians would be horrified by such a suggestion. One cannot help but wonder if sincere people who call themselves Christians may be holding to different Christs or different religions altogether. Of course, it is possible, but how does this apply here? Is this what characterizes the surviving remnants of religion in the West? Christ said that there would be false Christs who would appear in the "last days" which very well may apply to the day in

which we live (Matt. 24:5, Mark. 13:21-22). There is the Christ who
is "accepting" of homosexual activity and another Christ who hates
homosexual activity. There is the Christ who loves homosexuals and
the Christ who hates homosexuals. There is the Lord Jesus Christ
who sits on a throne and calls nations to repentance, and then there
is the Jesus who accepts everybody just the way they are. Then, there
is another Jesus who bears more resemblance to a Mexican drug lord
named "Jesus." He makes people feel good.

WILL THE REAL JESUS PLEASE STAND UP?

The question posed is a serious one. Would Jesus tattoo Leviticus
19:28 on his left thigh? Forty years ago, the answer to the question
would hardly be debatable, if the question was ever asked. However,
those who are still associated with the Christian faith today are
interested in these sorts of questions, in part because this is the age
of apostasy. Very little of the Christian faith has survived in Europe
(at least if you believe the news reports and the statistical studies
covering church attendance and baptisms), and North American
Christianity is fading rapidly. Families who do not want to apostatize
from the faith still want to know what the faith looks like. Our faith
does more than assent to propositions, such as the historical fact of
Christ's resurrection. Persons who believe in the resurrection will
live in a manner that reflects that belief.

The organized Christian church in the West has very much unraveled.
Most protestant sects (Mennonite, Episcopal, Presbyterian,
Methodist, Baptist, Lutheran, etc.) have compromised on homosexual
weddings, female pastors, evolution, and a hundred other corrupting
apostasies. Would these churches make similar mistakes regarding
other cultural elements including motion pictures, popular music,
clothing, body piercing, and tattoos? Which cultural forms represent
apostasy and which represent a commitment to orthodoxy? These
are important questions to those of us who want our children and
grandchildren to be part of the Christian church in the year 2060.
What would the real Jesus think of Lady Gaga's music? What would
the real Jesus think of the evangelical pastor who tattooed a dragon
across his back and neck? Would the real Jesus wear a Broncos

jersey? Why didn't Joseph of Arimathea cremate the real Jesus? If a tree is known by its fruits, at what point does a culture reveal the fruits of complete apostasy from the Christian faith?

Much has changed in just fifty years. The facádes came down in the last half century and cultural expressions now more closely reflect the true worldview commitment at heart. Until the middle of the 20th century, England and America still "looked" Christian on the outside, even though the foundational view of knowledge and reality within these nations had changed significantly. By the turn of the 21st century, most of these facádes had come down. Now that the Western apostasy is in full force in Europe and North America, many have adopted a different worldview. They have taken on a man-centered epistemology, metaphysic, and ethical perspective. They may still call themselves "Christians," but their basic worldview is humanist at its core. Shifting worldviews eventually yield different cultural accretions. Naturally, a post-Christian world will come to *look* post-Christian as the years advance. That is what we would expect.

Francis Schaeffer famously remarked that one gets a worldview like he gets the measles. The fellow is not sure how he picked it up, but sure enough, he has the measles. If the doctor were to examine him, certain spots on the skin would clearly indicate he has the disease. If the patient bears symptoms of the measles, it is a good bet that he has the measles. In a similar sense, a culture provides external evidence of the disease that ravages the body of society. In order to correctly identify a worldview, it is helpful to study culture and better understand connections between culture and worldview. In many ways, the culture is the best and only way to correctly identify a worldview. For one thing, people are not always truthful in their confessions. They may say that they believe in God and the resurrection of Christ, for example, but in life practice they deny it. Thus, it is better to examine a man's culture than his stated beliefs. Far too many claim the name of Christ, but deny Him by their works. When Christ speaks of works, He is referring to habits, lifestyle, priorities, assorted applications of law, and in a word, culture.

Most Christians today get a little "Jesus" at church, but they pick up their worldview from their school classroom and their iPods. They usually do not realize that they picked up the "measles" in Hollywood and Nashville, but that is in fact what happens. Usually, cultural leaders self-consciously define their worldview first, and then purposely translate their worldview into cultural expression. However, most people adopt the cultural forms of the leaders first, and then more or less consciously realize the worldview they have adopted.

The business of analyzing and interpreting culture is not an easy one—it is more difficult than diagnosing a medical condition. From the outset, I would caution the reader not to oversimplify the process. My purpose in this book is to lay out the basic definitions and guidelines by which we can discern the connections between culture and worldview. This, I trust, will be far more useful to the average Christian than to produce yet another book dissecting worldviews.

For the purposes of this book, culture shall be defined as the life of family and community. Culture is manifest through language, literature, dress, manners, music, motion pictures, architecture, art, and work.

THE POWER OF CULTURE

It was an unusual phone call taken by the MTV executive office somewhere in the early 1990s. The premier of China was on the line and he wanted to speak to MTV's Chief Executive Officer. "What are you going to do to my country?" he asked.

Forget the military strength of one of the largest nations on planet earth. When it came to changing a nation's social and political systems, there was no better way to do it than by the powerful cultural influences of music and the visual medium.

After all of China's tyrannical forced abortions, infanticides, and sterilizations over three decades to support the one-child policy, China's birth rate finally dropped to 1.58 by 2011. For South Korea however, the process was much more simple. Their access to Western culture enabled a swifter and far less interventionist approach, resulting in a contraction of the birth rate from 6.0 to 1.24 between 1960 and 2011.[1] This poses an interesting question. Does a political state influence the average person as much as do music videos, soap operas, movie stars, and Pop music? It is doubtful. South Korea had ready access to Western education and culture. Although this nation had been more influenced by Christian missionary work than any other Far Eastern nation (and arguably, more than any other nation in the world), the ideas conveyed by Western culture outweighed anything Western missionaries had achieved.[2]

Another example of the powerful impact of secular media on culture reveals itself in the case of recent immigrants to America. Persecuted Christians from Russia and the Slavic countries flocked into America when the iron curtain came down in the early 1990s. I have met with thousands of these Christian refugees over the last decade or so. Many of these families are amazed at the powerful, toxic nature of American popular culture or teen culture in the lives of their sons and daughters. They had no idea that the American culture would be more dangerous to their families than what they had experienced under the Communists.

Suppose a Christian father was given the choice between exposing his child to atheist teachers for six hours a day for five years, and exposing his child to a Katy Perry-saturated teen culture for six hours a day for five years, I judge he should choose the former. Most kids don't pay attention to their teachers in school anyway. The worldviews of young people are generally dictated more by Pop culture and peers than by their teachers.

I'll never forget the day that the box office released the movie of the second Narnia tale. I took my children to watch *Prince Caspian*. Towards the end of the movie, we were shocked to witness the apparently innocuous, though romantic kiss between Susan and Caspian. The film only netted a PG rating. The romantic interest supplied an unnecessary, gratuitous element to the story. However, that is not what bothered me the most. Any reader of the Narnia tales would know that there is no possibility of a future relationship between Caspian and Susan. As the story ends, Caspian leaves the scene forever, never to pursue the romantic interest again. To the audience, it is clear that Caspian is having a little sexual fun with a girl outside of the marriage covenant.

Exacerbating the problem for the *Caspian* scene was the social context into which the romantic interlude was introduced. Before entering the theater, I had read a USA Today report that 95% of Americans getting married confess to having experienced premarital sexual relations.[3] How does a once Christianized society descend to these depths? While it is true that premarital fornication has always existed, the incidence hovered around a percent or two until the 20th century (and more specifically—until after the 1950s). Now, premarital sexual activity is practically normative. What used to be considered dysfunctional and socially deconstructive becomes the new normal. Moreover, the last few virgins left are 14, 15, and 16-year-old evangelical children who have yet to experience a romantic relationship without the intention of marriage. Yet these were the children flocking to watch *Prince Caspian*, not to exclude my own children. Hollywood's producers understand that they have yet to capture the 5% of Americans who are steadfastly holding to the old Christian morality, and this is the way to do it. While it is possible that some producers are not fully aware of the agenda they promote, it is hard to believe that all of them are ignorant of the cultural significance of their cinematic creations.

POPULAR CULTURE IS POWER CULTURE

Everything changed in the 20th century. The 19th century farmer boy in upstate New York was not rocking out to Elvis Presley and Michael Jackson. For 5900 years, most children were far more influenced by their own parents, or by the Folk culture developed in their local communities, than by a cultural machine centered in a place called Hollywood or Nashville. The farmer boy had never heard of MTV, Lady Gaga, *Star Wars*, *Two and a Half Men*, hook-ups, shack-ups, iPods, and online pornography. If he wanted to find a Proverbs 7 sort of harlot, he would have had to ride his horse for two or three days, and he may have found one in New York City. Today, 80% of young men, 18-25 years old are hooked on online pornography, at a frequency of weekly or monthly visits.[4] Hard as it may be for a young person to imagine today, there was no television, no YouTube, and no Top 40 songs for over 5900 years of world history. Pa played his violin during the long winter evenings as the family gathered around the fireplace. The local community showed up for the barn dance on Saturday night, and that was about it. Cultural patterns developed in a decentralized context. Pastors and parents acted as the cultural leaders in each community with every successive generation.

Popular culture is power culture. These cultural systems enter almost every home in the country by way of hundreds of 50,000-watt transmitters. This now provides for far more energy and reach than one man could ever produce even when speaking very loudly at a public event (such as the Superbowl). Expensive satellites beam signals into every home, whether it be in the most remote village in Ecuador, a farm town in Iowa, or an apartment in downtown Chicago. They all receive the same message, the same standard of "cool," the same form of music, the same standards of morality (or lack of it), and the same role models in the same dysfunctional movie stars and singers. None of this would have come to pass without the centralization of media control in the cultural capitals of Hollywood and Nashville. The limited accessibility of radio and television station licenses has also contributed to the centralization of media. Newspapers and other media created stars out of entertainment and sports figures, providing objects of worship for the masses. Actors and musicians appeared larger than life, thanks to camera angles, movie scripts, and the "fame machines" of radio, television, and print media. The people ate it up, and Hollywood and Nashville were happy to provide gruel for their appetite. Thus, Michael Jackson and The Beatles replaced Pa and his fiddle in the homes of South Dakota farm towns.

In the music industry today, the top five recording artists lead the way for the top 40 artists in the nation. These, in turn set the cultural standards for the top 100 artists, who will set the cultural standards for the lesser artists in the genre who provide cultural guidance for the Christian Contemporary artists, as well as a million fourteen-year-old star wannabes in every neighborhood from here to Manhattan, Kansas. The modern cultural milieu turned into a semi-monolithic pyramid capturing billions of people in its web. To question the morality or worldview of it would be to suggest that human nature is something depraved, which is unthinkable for modern man. Most Christians prefer to keep culture in the category *adiophora*—"things indifferent"—and assume it is harmless or of little influence.

CULTURAL AND SOCIAL REVOLUTIONS

Popular culture would never have achieved such a high degree of influence had it not been for the disappearance of family culture and Folk culture. Without a social revolution, there would have been no cultural revolution. Without age-segregated high schools and the disappearance of the family farm economy, there would have been no Elvis Presley, Michael Jackson, or Katy Perry. As fathers left the family farm, and mothers disappeared from the home, children were drawn into a different social system with its own culture. Popular culture shapes youth culture. It is a culture more highly influenced by Miley Cyrus and Justin Bieber than by Ma and Pa. Media, social media, children's literature, schools, peer groups, church youth programs, and extra-curricular activities have worked together to produce this new socio-cultural order. The sheer power of this system over a child's social and cultural development is astounding. With the exception of certain immigrant communities, fragments of the homeschooling movement, and a few family economies, popular culture virtually consumes modern society. Even these exceptional movements have been largely incapable of overcoming the impact of Pop culture. The cultural war is more powerful and more fundamental than the political battles.

POPULAR CULTURE TURNS DESTRUCTIVE

What does popular culture do with all of this centralized power? The answer should be obvious. When the top five performing artists in the nation are unequivocal post-modernists like Miley Cyrus, Lady

Gaga, Katy Perry, Taylor Swift, Kacey Musgraves, or a band that hammers out an explicit description of a rape in 4.5 minutes, one wonders how quickly these worldviews sink into the consciousness of the masses. This transition seems to be accelerating now, as society morphs from civilized, to decadent, to nihilist. When Kurt Cobain committed suicide in the early 1990s, a nihilist worldview controlled about 25% of the chart toppers. There was only a fifteen year spread between the decadence of Madonna and the celebration of meaninglessness, self-mockery, and sexual nihilism of Lady Gaga. Miley Cyrus moved from nice to naughty to nihilist inside of about four years. There were thirty years between Doris Day's hit song "How Much is That Doggie in the Window?" and Madonna's "Like a Virgin." Ten years later, Katy Perry encouraged fourteen-year-olds to lesbian sexuality. Now Lady Gaga, Britney Spears, Kacey Musgraves, and the entire crew traverse from the span of decadence to nihilism with almost every hit song. In the same breath, they both celebrate and mock sado-masochism, self-adulation, and all forms of sexual decadence.

One would think that a few sane people would be a little concerned about the popular song, "Blurred Lines," which dominated the charts in the latter half of 2013. This hit song spoke in positive (or semi-ambivalent) support of sexual assault, to include explicit pornographic detail. That this foul piece of work should make it to the number one position on music charts in twenty-six major countries around the world is of no small historical significance. We've come a long way from Elvis Presley's "Hound Dog" and Michael Jackson's "Billie Jean." This is what the collapse of a civilization looks like. We must not ignore this outcome. To ignore the destructive power of culture is to be consumed by it. These things should more than catch our attention. They should radically transform the way that Christian families look at popular culture. I have monitored popular cultural offerings since I worked as a disc jockey on various radio formats in the 1980s. The top songs in the nation express the socially destructive, suicidal impulse more consistently, openly and honestly than ever before. We shudder to think what would follow the outlandish nihilism of Lady Gaga and Miley Cyrus. What more vivid picture of sexual nihilism could be found than Billy Ray Cyrus' daughter swinging nude on a wrecking ball in a recent music video? Where will these stars take the world in the next twenty years? What happens next? Will more than one billion people commit suicide at the same time, when they finally comprehend the full implications of the culture they have embraced?

Cultures reveal the hearts of men, and by nature, men's hearts are "deceitful above all things and desperately wicked" (Jer. 17:9). This does not mean that all culture is hopelessly perverted. After 2000 years of faithful discipleship and implementation of Christ's Great Commission, it is impossible to miss something of Christ's redemptive work permeating human culture around the globe. Yet, the Western world is still in all-out apostasy, and that is a game changer. The leaven of apostasy has spread to every developed nation. This makes modern culture more difficult to interpret, in that there are both apostatizing trajectories and Christian roots intertwined within Western culture.

As I walked through the streets of downtown Melbourne, Australia last year, I was transfixed as I observed the clash of old and new, the constructive and the destructive within the culture. I witnessed neatly dressed school children walking down streets layered in graffiti. There seemed to be multiple strains of culture in conflict. These well groomed school children who attend nice British public schools and Christian schools are listening to Lady Gaga on their iPods. Among the British nations there is still something left that sustains civilization, but there is also that which is destroying it. America has very little heritage left to preserve the culture, perhaps even less than the nations still under the influence of the Queen.

"My Grandfather's Clock" was the most popular song in the nation in 1876, selling over a million copies in sheet music.[5] Today, almost 130 years later, the most popular hits refer to mothers as female dogs and speak freely of raping people. This is called a "cultural shift." It would be difficult to interpret what is happening in a culture if we monitored it for only a year or two. But over ten years, the changes become perceptible, and a hundred years is plenty of time to make the call. The average person is as unaware of cultural developments, as the frog that sits in the slowly boiling water is hardly aware of his circumstance. If the temperature rises at one degree per year, the frog will not realize his predicament.

CULTURE IS A RIVER

Certainly, it would be unfair to judge an artist's work by a single paint stroke or even a single painting, as it would be wrong to judge a director by a single movie scene. All art and culture must be seen in historical, social, and cultural context. All culture must be interpreted by its trajectory. Where is culture headed? In order to capture a sense of direction, we will need more than one datapoint. Multiple data points are made available over time, as the true nature of the heart is revealed. Whether it be your teenage son or Katy Perry (who was raised by a Christian pastor and admits to growing tired of singing "Amazing Grace"), the trajectory of the heart is eventually made clear.

Culture flows like a river, with occasional eddies and swirls. Take for example, the Contemporary Christian Music phenomenon of the last forty years. In the late 1960s, Larry Norman and a few other lesser names formed the genre out of the Rock n' Roll revolution of the day. It was a rivulet that spun off of the macro-stream of mass culture. Back in the 1980s, I organized concerts and worked as a disc jockey in the CCM genre on the California central coast. The industry was fraught with scandal. Larry Norman himself went through two divorces and married Randy Stonehill's ex-wife. World Magazine reported Norman having fathered a child with an Australian woman during a 1988 tour.[6] One of the early "mothers" of contemporary Christian music, Marsha Stevens, exited the closet as a lesbian in 1979. The CCM industry is filled with sordid stories of adultery and divorce (including familiar names like Sandi Patty, Amy Grant, John Talbot, and Jaci Velasquez). If the Christian contemporary culture left the mainstream flow of popular culture, it did not differentiate by much. Do Christ's words apply?

"Ye shall know them by their fruits. Do men gather grapes of thorns, or figs of thistles? Even so every good tree bringeth forth good fruit;

but a corrupt tree bringeth forth evil fruit." (Matt. 7:16-17)

The truth value of such words demands our constant consideration and appropriate application to cultural leaders.

Bands like Stryper make it practically impossible to detect any clear distinction between the "Christian" element and the macro-culture. Their latest album released in 2011 called *The Covering* featured songs from Black Sabbath, Scorpion, Iron Maiden, and Judas Priest along with a "Christian" song tacked on entitled "God." If life is an "illusion," as Black Sabbath insists in their song "Heaven and Hell", why do we need mercy, as Stryper testifies in their little appendix to the album? Essentially, Stryper does little to counter the basic metaphysical perspective represented by the Heavy Metal genre, except to offer a weak suggestion that some god or Jesus figure might help us along the way. Stryper is a prime example of thorough Christian synthesis.

The Contemporary Christian Music culture turned mainstream in the 1990s. An Ellison Research study found that the use of CCM doubled in churches between 1998 and 2004, impacting some 74% of Christian churches in America.[7] Those numbers would be higher today. The influence of CCM upon every Christian denomination (almost without exception), is truly remarkable and is not to be ignored in the study of the 21st century Christian church. This makes for an interesting study of culture. Will a marginal departure from the mainstream culture redeem the music genre? Does this movement represent a true shift in worldview, or will this branch merely parallel the main river and continue flowing towards the Niagara Falls with the rest of it? Years from now, we will see the definitive effects of the work of Randy Stonehill, Larry Norman, and Marsha Stevens on the church of Jesus Christ. Did they save Christianity in a secular humanist age, or did they secularize Christianity in an age of apostasy? The jury is still out; time will tell.

If you visit the fifty to one hundred radio stations available on the AM and FM dials in any major market, you will find that over 90% of the selections represent a fairly narrow cultural experience. You may find one Classical or Jazz station, a 40s Big Band station, and a few news talk stations. Other than that, the cultural idiom is popular music in the form of Rock n' Roll. Even the Country-Folk formats have slowly morphed into the popular form between 1970 and the present day. On one hand, it is not difficult to follow the macro cultural trends. There is however, more going on than the Top 40 offerings. Despite the seemingly monolithic character of the popular culture and worldview represented by media today, there are hundreds, if not thousands, of cultural variants, musical genres, and theological variations in our day. These are the swirls, eddies, and rivulets that form in the cultural river. Objectively, some are better than others. The "contemporary" Folk style of Michael Card is a far cry from that of Stryper, for example. Nobody would disagree that the family-friendly movie productions from the Kendrick brothers (*Facing the Giants, Fireproof,* and *Courageous*) makes for a better offering than *Two and a Half Men*, despite Angus T. Jones' involvement. In the fall of 2012, actor Angus Jones encouraged a Christian television audience not to watch this "filth."

> "Please stop filling your head with filth. Please. People say it's just entertainment... Watch out... A lot of people don't like to think how deceptive the enemy is. He's been doing this a lot longer than any of us have been around... You cannot be a true, God-fearing person and be on a show like that."[8]

Two and a Half Men may be the raunchiest television program on air, routinely making light of bestiality and sexual orgies (and netting the worst ratings from the Parent's Television Counsel). Eventually, Jones quit the show despite his influential position and $8 million per year remuneration.

Serious attempts at cultural reformation are made every day by well-meaning Christian artists and producers, and these efforts ought to be recognized for what they are worth—though it is not easy to judge their long term value. Will Good Newz Tattooz sanctify the somewhat questionable, if not patently pagan, practice of tattooing for the modern church? Will Pat Boone's Heavy Metal album *No More Mr. Nice Guy* represent a reformation in the genre to the glory of God? Or is it just another frivolous novelty of little consequence?

Will Miss USA Runner-Up Carrie Prejean (2009), or Miss America Teresa Scanlan (2011), both professing Christians, lead a cultural shift for women in the direction of Christian modesty, meekness, and piety? (1 Tim. 2:9-10). How will the Miss USA bikini competition on national television help with this? Would a professing Christian's involvement as an actor in the sit-com *Two and a Half Men* really offer some "salt and light" in a decadent culture? These are the sorts of questions that serious Christians are asking themselves in the first part of the 21st century. If we are pressing for a thoroughly authentic faith from the inside out, then what is the essential value of these cultural offerings? Where lies the heart of the 21st century Christian, and how is it impacting culture?

BASELINE AND TRAJECTORY

Since culture is the product of human activity that reflects the condition of the human heart, we can interpret the condition of the heart by observing a body of cultural work over a period of time. We must therefore consider both *baseline* and *trajectory*. What is true of an individual life is true of the culture. We all claim a background, for better or worse. Everyone starts somewhere. Whether you are the son of a prostitute from Brooklyn, the son of a tribal chieftain in the Congo, or a daughter of a Christian missionary, you have a heritage. This is your baseline. Communities and entire civilizations always work from baselines. For example, the culture of a public junior high school in a small farm town in South Dakota will be different from the culture of a Japanese junior high school in Kobe, Japan. The Christian civilization in 16th-century England will be different from that which is represented in twenty-first century Chicago. In the Parable of the Talents, Christ describes baseline as the principle investment issued to the three men by the householder. One man received a single talent, another received two talents, and a third received five (Matt. 25:14-30). All of them began with something, and two of them produced return on the investment and one did not.

Cultural trajectory is defined as the direction and force with which an individual, family, or community takes their cultural heritage. Do they improve on what they have received, or not? Is there any advancement in their cultural expressions towards reflecting what is true, right, and beautiful—or not? When missionaries arrived in Hawaii in the 19th century, they removed the sacred significance of the hula dance and taught the women to put on clothing while performing the dance, since both genders had been performing the dance topless. However, following the 1960s Hawaiian culture reversed and the clothes came off. Now, the political and cultural leaders in the state are turning back the clock and reintroducing pagan ideologies and practices as preferable to the Western Christian influence. Much of this is encouraged by the Western apostasy. Hawaiian culture is on a new trajectory now.

If we want to know which Christians survived the Great Apostasy of the twenty-first century, we must watch their trajectories. Baselines are varied, but trajectories will tell the story. When Country music star Carrie Underwood began her career with the hit song, "Jesus Take the Wheel," we weren't sure which Jesus she was talking about. However, after years of hit songs and personal testimonies extolling the virtues of homosexuality, fornication, and feminism, we are left with no doubt as to the heart commitments of Carrie Underwood.[9] Culture is trajectory. The American evangelical world was thrilled with the release of the Soul Surfer motion picture in 2011, only to discover that Carrie Underwood played the role of the youth pastor, and the girls in bikinis were less than helpful for the 14-year old boys sitting in the theater.

The trajectory for Western popular culture should not be too difficult to follow. Fifty years after Patty Page issued her hit song, "How Much is That Doggie in the Window?," the masses aren't buying her albums anymore. They prefer Eminem's albums where he refers to his mother as a female dog, and where rape and homosexuality are more accepted themes. At this point in history, the change is rapid. Popular culture did not change at this breakneck pace between 1750 and 1800. During the first Grammy Award Ceremonies in 1959, the Song of the Year award went to Jimmie Driftwood's "Battle of New Orleans," and the academy focused more on classical performances. The 2014 Grammys, however, offered a Satanic orgy, in which a lesbian priestess officiated 33 homosexual weddings and

Katy Perry served as the witch offering her sacrifices to the "Dark Horse."[10] Christian apostasy has become an accepted theme, and this was especially pronounced with Grammy Award Winner for Best Country Song, Kacey Musgraves. In her recent release "Follow Your Arrow", she encourages her listeners to lesbianism and more apostasy from "self-righteous" churches. Her mockery is laced with profanity. Back in 1969, Bobby Bare wasn't brave enough to offer explicit approval of apostasy in his "Margie's at the Lincoln Park Inn." Rather, he described Christian hypocrisy in stark and explicit form, somewhat nonchalantly. Taking a 40-year perspective, the trajectory of the Pop and Country music genres should be obvious.

THE STANDARD

Naturally, modern relativists will reject my underlying assumption that some cultures are objectively better than others. Romantics like Jean-Jacques Rousseau felt that the pagan cannibals untouched by Western Christianity constituted the ideal culture. But true relativists deny the use of the terms "better than" or "worse than." They hesitate to criticize any culture whatsoever, with perhaps the one exception of Hitler's Third Reich. This does not reflect the Christian worldview, however. There must be a standard for what is true and right, and one either seeks to uphold the standard or reject it. At the end of a man's life, he has either created a body of work that supports a Christian world and life view, or he has detracted from it.

Nonetheless, there is something subjective about my approach, since every artist starts from a different baseline. Take, for example, the young man raised in the slums who tries to morph a Christian music form out of a model developed by inner city gangs. Contrast this with another young man who is a descendent of multiple generations of Christians, and raised on music written by Christians, but decides to write his music based on the musical style developed by inner city gangs. These two young men work off of very different baselines and produce diametrically opposite trajectories. The man with a strong Christian heritage abandons what he has inherited, while the other young man is working with what he knows. When a Christian father weighs in on his daughter's potential suitors, he is faced with something similar. Should his daughter marry the pastor's son who is rebelling against his own father's faith? Or would it be better if she married a genuinely repentant ex-pagan who was raised on the other side of the tracks?

The Halloween festival makes for another interesting example. Technically, the word is of Christian origin, a derivation of "All Hallow's Eve." It had nothing to do with Freddie, Jason, and the Slasher movies. For thousands of years, the world celebrated the Day of the Dead on or around October 31st. The Day of the Dead began after the worldwide flood, when many of the descendants of Noah turned their backs on the true story of God's judgment upon a world that had rejected His laws. So they chose to commemorate the event in a different way. Rather than celebrating God's mercy on their ancestors (Noah and his family), they spent their time lamenting God's judgment on everybody else. Many pagan peoples around the globe kept the Day of the Dead until the Christian age dawned. Then, as Christians sought to remember the faithful men and women who served Jesus Christ under severe persecutions, All Hallow's Eve became the default holiday for a thousand years or so. As time went on, however, the Day of the Dead made a comeback. During the apostasy of the 20th century, almost everyone forgot about All Hallow's Eve, in favor of the Day of the Dead. Recently, some news sources report that there are more Americans celebrating Halloween (as the Day of the Dead), than those celebrating Easter. A casual observer will come to the same conclusions. I walked through a department store in October of 2013, and found that about a third of the store was dedicated to selling Day of the Dead paraphernalia.

There is an interesting irony here. In the Christian age, believers retained the holiday but changed the name and the meaning of the day. In today's post-Christian era, the Christian name is been retained ("Halloween") but the old significance returns. At this point, my readers should see the tug-of-war going on between Christianity and paganism. Modern civilizations are thrust into a life and death struggle over what direction the culture is to take next.[11]

THE GOAL

If Christ's mandate was that His followers disciple the nations by teaching them to observe His commandments, then it logically follows that Christians are commissioned to culture change (Matt. 28:18-20). When the Gospel first came to the New Hebrides in the 1880s, Margaret Paton (John Paton's wife) told of the chaos that went on in the early Sunday worship services.[12] Apparently, the natives were bringing their pigs and chickens with them to the service, and they made quite a racket! The natives knew that if they left their animals or any of their valuables at home, they would be robbed. As the missionaries inculcated a Christian system of law and life and orderly government, respect for property was instituted. Only then did the people begin to leave their pigs and chickens at home on Sunday mornings. This is a simple example of a culture change that comes about when the Gospel makes it into the warp and woof of a nation.

To say that the Christian missionary must adapt the message to fit the culture is legitimate as long as he works off of the baseline of any cultural system. However, many Christian ministries see no real need to change the culture by setting new trajectories. Thus, they never quite embrace the clear commission Christ gave to His apostles. All true followers of Christ will set out to change every aspect of human culture, including the language.

Several years ago, I viewed the dramatization of the Jim Elliot story presented in the motion picture *End of the Spear*. It was confusing to me. Why did the producers choose to use an outspoken homosexual as the lead actor? Why were the missionaries stripping off their clothes as they came into contact with the Auca natives? What other Christian leaders and missionaries over the last 2,000 years would have advocated such contextualization? It is hard to imagine John G. Paton, David Brainerd, or Patrick of Ireland stripping off their clothes for the benefit of the natives, and hiring homosexuals to preach their message for them. In an effort to be relevant, some Christians will surrender everything and abandon the commission. They are content to leave a pagan culture at its baseline. They drive no new trajectories. More fundamentally, they fail to apply the law of God from the outset to such matters as modesty, sexuality, and body mutilation. They also fail to correctly interpret the meaning of native cultural symbols (religious rites, food offered to idols, etc.) Of course, many evangelicals argue that they are willing to do anything to "get people saved." In the neo-evangelical mind, this means a separation of justification and sanctification. Salvation *is* justification, and does not include sanctification for them. This separation in the modern salvation message has destroyed the Christian Gospel and rendered it powerless to accomplish Christ's commission.

LANGUAGE AND BIBLE TRANSLATION

Cultural transformation must impact Bible translations as well, for all native languages are formed around defective worldviews. For example, the word used for "God" in Japanese Bibles is "kami." The word itself is incapable of conveying the biblical idea of God, because it connotes something else in the Japanese mind. It is a word used for the many spirits of demons, angels, false gods, and humans. When the Bible is translated into a native language for the first time, the translators are bound to the baseline, meaning that they must begin with the limited vocabulary and the limited conceptual reservoir contained in the native language itself. Over time the language must be made to adapt to the Christian worldview. With more teaching on biblical concepts and a robust biblical worldview, and as thousands of men and women are discipled over hundreds of years, new translations of the Bible will emerge that better reflect the true meaning contained in the Hebrew and Greek Bible.

The Hawaiian Pidgin Bible provides a colorful illustration of the limitation of language, using words most of us can understand. The Pidgin language is obviously constrained by vocabulary, cultural and linguistic connotations, and grammar (or lack of it). What follows is a section of the Pidgin translation from Matthew 13.

"Same day Jesus go outside da house, an sit down near da lake fo teach. Plenny peopo come aroun him, so he go inside one small boat, an sit down dea. Da peopo, dey stay standing on top da beach. He use plenny stories fo teach um. Dis wat he

say,"You guys hear da story bout da farma guy? He go plant
seed. He throw da seeds fo plant. Some fall down by da side a
da trail, an da birds go eat um up. Some fall down on top da
rocks wea ony had litto bit dirt. But dey grow up fast, cuz ony
litto bit dirt dea." (Matthew 13:1-4).[13]

The reader may be impressed by the simplicity of the language, in
that the vocabulary provides a limited basis for conveying biblical
ideas. Whether the problem is rooted in paganism or in a weakened
Hawaiian education system is hard to say. Chances are, the early
Bibles used in 19th century Hawaii reflected a more accurate
translation and gravitas. Over the last century, we have witnessed a
deconstruction of language, especially among certain subcultures in
English-speaking countries.

Moreover, efforts to disciple the nations living under colonialism
(and the African slave trade that fed into America) were probably
curtailed at points. The failure to disciple will always produce
the failure of Christian culture. Where men fail to disciple other
men by faithful daily instruction in the Word of God, there will
be no solid Christian men to lead family, church, and culture in
subsequent generations. Whether it be South Africa, Hawaii, or the
American inner city, one will often find churches emptied of men,
with not enough male pastors and elders. Too much Christian work
during the last century has been shallow, short term, and ineffective,
especially in its attempts to reach men.

If we are serious about discipling entire nations, there must be a
willingness to dig in for the long haul. Over several hundred years
of careful discipleship and disciplined education in Greek, Hebrew,
Latin, English, History, Biblical Theology, Systematic Theology,
Hermeneutics, and life application, peoples from any nation would
see slow but steady transformation in their families, churches, and
cultures. In time, they would develop their own spoken and written
languages that would better serve as a vehicle to carry the Word of
God. Thus, the people group that is discipled gains an understanding
of God's revelation which then shifts their worldview towards a
Christian way of thinking. This shift produces a transformation of

language, which in turn produces new translations of the Bible. With better translations of the Bible will come a sharpened conception of a biblical world and life view, and on it goes. This is the cycle by which minds are renewed and transformed according to the will of God (Rom. 12:1-2), and civilizations become Christian.

2: Culture Changers
Isolation or Impact?

We have already argued the case for the Great Commission and its impact on culture. Nonetheless, the question of involvement is not cut and dried. The decision to engage or disengage in culture will result in either separatism or puritanism. The Puritans faced the same question, as did the early Church Fathers. While some Christians rush into Hollywood to "make a difference," others produce their own films and participate in Christian independent film festivals held around the country. Take for example, the Christian young man who gets his four year degree in Graphic Arts and hires on with a film company in Hollywood. His first project involves a slasher film in which all the characters break God's commandments with impunity, and there is no meaningful distinction between good and evil, the good guys and bad guys. Nonetheless, our Christian friend still "makes an impact" for Jesus when he gets to add A.D. after the copyright date at the end of the credits in the last few frames of the film. This, I am afraid, is the cultural contribution of far too many Christians in the entertainment world. They want to dedicate their lives to making an impact, but their participation in ungodly forms of media simply furthers the cause of an ungodly culture, year in and year out. Could the young man have produced more "talents" for the kingdom of God and His righteousness outside Hollywood rather than inside Hollywood?

There is a point at which our efforts towards cultural transformation reduce to something like spraying a little perfume over a cesspool in a futile effort to "make a difference." As a young man, I remember my mother telling me before I left the home: "If more of them is rubbing off on you than you on them, you have probably placed yourself in the wrong context in relation to the world." There is some wisdom here for all of us. We each have one life to live, and we each make individual choices concerning how we will use our time and resources. Our primary measure for success in life is not money and fame, but the kingdom of God and His righteousness (Matt. 6:33). Where righteousness prevails in our lives and in the institutions with which we have some contact, where our obedience is perfected and the disobedience of the nations corrected (2 Cor. 10:5-6), we have made good use of our talents.

People want to think of fame as relating directly to impact, although there is little correlative relationship between them. A great number of obscure saints have performed great and noble deeds, though they are hardly recognized for their accomplishments (Eccl. 9:14-15). In other instances, promising Christians obtained a little influence in politics and culture, and then promptly compromised their faith and used their influence for the cause of the wrong kingdom—the kingdom of darkness. This scenario may be more the rule than the exception today. Like Carrie Underwood, they begin their career singing "Jesus Take the Wheel," and spend the rest of their lives advocating homosexual marriage.[1] When many Christian teachers enter the public schools, instead of teaching the fear of God as the beginning of knowledge, they do just the opposite. They teach children *not* to fear God. In so doing, they contribute to the ongoing demise of the Christian faith in academics, politics, and the marketplace.

In the present age of rampant apostasy, Christians in the West struggle for some relevance. We elbow into the conversation, because we want to be heard. We instinctively act so as to impact the culture. We want to be salt and light within the culture around us. But there are serious temptations and stumbling blocks that would present themselves to us in the venture. On one hand, we are tempted to pessimism, especially when humanist secularism is on the rise. This often ends in retreat and total isolation. Yet we are also tempted to blur the line between the antithesis and the thesis by synthesizing with the culture under the banner of relevance. Often, this happens incrementally over a lifetime of work. An artist may begin with a strong Christian testimony, but then proceeds to trade his principles for fame, money, and "impact," which in the end produces less for the kingdom of God—no obedience matured, no disobedience avenged, and no thoughts brought into captivity to the obedience of Christ (2 Cor. 10:4-6). This story is far too common among Christians in the ongoing saga of Western apostasy.

On the other hand, it is a different kind of faithlessness that retreats into total isolation. It is faithlessness that refuses to maintain God's ethical standard against the antithesis of the day and resorts to a pattern of compromise with the world. It is faithlessness that settles for a pessimistic eschatological outlook. Sadly, too much of this faithlessness has characterized "conservative" Christianity generation after generation since the 1800s. This is simply another mark of apostasy.

THE BOTTOM LINE

If the whole duty of man is to fear God, love God, and keep His commandments, then this is also the basis for all Christian culture. Any culture reflecting some standard of righteousness will be a Christian culture, assuming that Christians derive their worldview outlook from divine truth as revealed through Scripture. Augustine draws the clear distinction between the city of God and the city of Man on this very point.

> "Let the desire of glory [or man's praise], be surpassed by the love of righteousness... for so hostile is this vice to pious faith, if the love of glory be greater in the heart than the fear or love of God, that the Lord said, 'How can ye believe, who look for glory from one another and do not seek the glory which is from God alone?'"[2]

Where there is some fear of God and obedience to God's standards of righteousness, there will be good culture. All else will pass away with the world and its lusts (1 John. 2:17).

COMMON GRACE

We should always consider where the influence of the fear of God
has penetrated the world's cultures. For example, it is possible that
the Jews influenced Japanese Shintoism thousands of years ago,
given the many parallels between the Shinto temple and worship
in the Old Testament temple, however perverted it became over the
centuries. Buddhist moralisms render some shadowy reflections of
Old Testament law, at points. The Muslim religion is a weak spin-off
of 7th century Judaism and Christianity. To negate the influence
of thousands of years of Christianity upon the world (even within
nations that are professedly non-Christian), is to minimize the work
of Christ. Thus, we must acknowledge that God's common grace
sends its tentacles into every field of art, music, science, literature,
and human endeavor. Where there was advancement in human
culture, there were traceable roots of biblical law and Christian faith
at work. Where human culture devolved, there was apostasy from
the faith and the subsequent corruption of demonic deceptions.

THE WORLD VS. CHRIST

There is some confusion among Christians concerning the nature
of the kingdom of God in the world. I believe the parable of the
Wheat and the Tares is helpful in understanding this relationship
(Matt. 13:24-30). In Jesus' parable, the wheat and the tares grow
together in the field until the end of the world. Jesus specifically
defines the field as being the world (vs. 38), and forbids a Christian
"jihad" (vs. 29). It is important to realize that the field is the world—
not the church. Yet, by the end of the parable, the angels reap the
wheat and the tares "out of the kingdom" (vs. 41). Evidently, the
field (the world) has become the kingdom of God by the end of the
parable.

There are two uses for the word "world" in the New Testament. While
God loves the "world" (John 3:16), we are also told, "Love not the
world, neither the things that are in the world" (1 John 2:14-16). The
world of lust and pride is to be eschewed by Christians. At the same
time, there is nothing wrong with loving and appreciating God's
created kosmos made up of human beings, animals, civil magistrates,

and economies. Nevertheless, we battle in the field of the world (the kosmos) against the influence of lust and pride.

This battle is everywhere, and it continues without respite. We engage this battle when we bring the fear of God and the principles of righteousness into the civil magistrate, media, art, culture, church, and family life. We are at all times and everywhere battling the lust of the flesh, the lust of the eyes, and the pride of life. What happens when the lust of the flesh and the pride of life dominate 98% of the institution? Would a Christian work for Playboy Magazine, or with some other element of the pornography industry, for example? When Hollywood or a political institution is consumed in flesh and pride, this may limit a Christian's ability to function therein. In some cases, he may exert influence over a smaller, more obscure division of the larger system. He may be pressed to man the emergency life raft centers while the Titanic is scraping the iceberg. He may be pressed to abandon the task of pumping out the engine rooms, and move on to saving a few lives in the emergency rafts. Whatever the case, he is still active and involved.

These two opposing allegiances battle over every square inch of the world (kosmos), the one is human pride and the other is Christ. It is impossible to avoid the battle in every home, church, business, and cultural institution. These two allegiances are, as Augustine puts it, "in this present world commingled, and as it were entangled together."[3] Some will work towards the end of ultimate separation but this is impossible and strictly forbidden in the parable of Christ (Matt. 13:29). Nonetheless, the wheat is still to be planted in the field such that the field becomes identified as the kingdom of God by the end. The wheat will inevitably dominate the field of the world, by the principle of the wheat (Christ) and not by the principle of the tare (human pride).

Thus, the field is defined relative to the varying levels of "tare-ishness" or "wheat-ishness" contained in the field. Because human society is, by definition, a connection among its various members, it is impossible for Christians not to influence the culture. The Corruptions Perception Index, for example, lays out the spectrum from the most honest to the most corrupt nations on earth. There is a reason that 13 out of the 16 most honest nations on earth have a Protestant heritage. Of the 21 most corrupt nations, five are Muslim, five are Animist, seven are Roman Catholic, and four are communist/atheist.[4] It is not that Christians currently make up 99% of the population of those nations with a Protestant heritage, but that Christian heritage and culture lingers through the generations. Even a minority can exert a strong influence upon the direction of a nation. Should a Christian look at his sales receipt and realize that he did not pay the full price for a product or service after the fact, he returns to the cash register and acknowledges the discrepancy. Each time this happens, his honesty bears salt and light influence upon the entire economy and culture of the field of the world. There is no escaping this reality.

Nevertheless, as Christians exert an influence on culture, they often face strong persecution. Typically, the persecution of God's people will result in the formation of a Christian ghetto of sorts, whether in the catacombs of Rome, the diaspora of the Mennonites, the Slavic Christians, or the Chinese Christians. Towards the end of the world, the camp of the saints appears separated and surrounded by the nations of the world (Rev. 20:9). An example of this in the Bible is found during the Israelites' sojourn in Goshen when there was a sharp economic separation from Egypt.

LONG TERM PROJECT

If the Great Commission was merely referring to a curtailed Gospel message and an emotional conversion experience, then the modern evangelical method would suffice. However, the Great Commission requires the missionary to instruct an indigenous people to observe whatsoever is commanded in the Word (Matt. 28:18-20). This includes teaching the testimonies, the laws of God, and the Book of the Proverbs, contained in the Old and New Testaments. Christians must be prepared to work for hundreds of years with the pagan tribes, in order to inculcate the life and law of Christ into the very fiber of the peoples.

Of course, any cultural advancement for God's kingdom will take a long time to come about. We ought never to think that perfection is our goal; no individual and no human institution will be perfected this side of glory. Utopian intentions are always dangerous. The Christian life comes about through fits and starts, and proceeds by ebb and flow.

Moreover, every new believer rescued from a pagan culture begins with the cultural tools of his early education and upbringing. He has to start somewhere. But as his worldview is transformed by the renewing of the mind and the discernment of the will of God (Rom. 12:1-2), that new believer begins to reform his culture, literature, art, architecture, and economy. This is a picture of the transformation from pagan life to that of a Christian.

But what happens when a Christian society is in apostasy? This is the wild card played by the present Western culture. We discover that we are a culture in regression. How does our current regressive culture form a baseline for Christian culture in the next generation? This question is worthy of consideration.

3: Hip-Hop
A Study In Form

Wikipedia lists seventy-four Christian Rap and Hip-Hop stars (as of 2013), who are all "making an impact" for Jesus with the Rap genre. Lecrae Moore is one of the best examples of a Christian engaging in the culture and attempting to make a difference. His recent album *Gravity* reached #3 on the Billboard 200 chart.[1] Recently Moore argued against "separatism" in an interview with Lifeway Christian Resources. "What we see a lot in the United States is the residue of what we call Christendom, where we know Christian culture but we really don't know the Christian Christ." Then, he decried those Christians who have "become separatists and say 'everything in the culture is bad.'"[2]

But, who is this Christian Christ? Might our relationship with Christ be evidenced in our culture or the way we live our lives? On the one hand, Lecrae rightly rejects the old cultural forms from the 1930s, 1940s, and 1950s that lack a faith core, and come across as hollow and meaningless to the new generation. By participating in the post-Christian cultural milieu, Lecrae hopes to make an impact with the real Christ. As the theory goes, if Christians borrow the new cultural forms developed in the post-Christian era, (whether Rock n' Roll, Heavy Metal, Rap, or Hip-Hop), and tack the name of Christ on to each of these forms, then perhaps some may be convinced to follow Christ. . . and this will result in discipled nations and Christianized culture.

The Hip-Hop genre he chose first emerged with discontented, disenfranchised, fatherless youth in the inner cities. Founder Afrika

Bambaataa, raised in the revolutionary cauldron of the 1960s black liberation movement, himself a gang warlord, named himself after a bloody African revolutionary. He vowed to use hip-hop to "draw angry kids out of gangs and form the Universal Zulu Nation."[3] Thus, Hip-Hop became a form in which to channel the anger of post-modern, disenfranchised, impoverished youth. This popular form is not to be ignored. Over the succeeding generation or two, a great deal of popular and Country music borrowed heavily from Hip-Hop for its cool hard edge and arrogant stark harshness. The genre provided an outlet for some of the most unimaginably evil expressions ever produced for public consumption. Some secular Hip-Hop artists would refer to their mothers as female dogs and most use a profane word that connotes rape with a nauseating frequency. It was the optimum form to express the anger and bitterness of young men without fathers, and the "gangsta rap" crowd used it effectively to this end.[4] Lecrae, however, will take doctrinally sound lyrics and place them in the Hip-Hop form. This might be a message preached in an orthodox church, yet it is inserted into a form of music created for a different purpose altogether. This does make for an interesting combination, and it is worth considering in this overview of modern culture.

From the outset, we should say that Christian culture cannot be directed by movies and music in a fundamental sense. Paul tells us that it is the "foolishness" of preaching that God uses to bring about the salvation of the nations (Rom. 10:13-16, 1 Cor. 1:21). If preaching is not changing worldviews and renewing minds, then all the Christians who are working so hard to impact culture will find their work irrelevant. If church services consist of forty minutes of music and twenty minutes of preaching once a week, it is doubtful that the nations will be discipled as a result. In fact, the other cultural expressions will become mere distractions to the youth, and the preaching will become increasingly passé.

If there is to be any positive change in culture and media, it will only happen via a shift in worldviews, and a fundamental change of mind: repentance. This usually comes by solid preaching and careful discipleship over many years. As one pastor stated: "I don't think one sermon does much good." That is because it takes twenty to thirty years of sound teaching before a change of culture emerges. If culture is defined as the externalization of a worldview, then one would expect the cultural form to adapt to the worldview over time. As language will adapt to the worldview it is attempting to communicate, so the music forms will adapt to the worldview it is attempting to communicate as well. Gradually, the true meaning of words and the worldview communicated will sink into the minds of those who hear the preaching and the music. Eventually, this must transform the cultural ethos (Rom. 12:1-2). Over time, Lecrae himself will become more self-conscious of a Christian world and life view and he will adapt his form to better suit his message. He'll possess a deeper comprehension of Trinitarian life; he'll learn something more of the fear of God, and express it better in his art. Perhaps the musical expression developed out of a discontented, rebellious, and fatherless culture is not the best suited form to convey the theology of the Bible.

In the 1970s and 1980s, we heard stories of men and women whose lives were changed by the Word of God, and who proceeded to burn their old "demon Metal" and "rape rap" albums. Yet, not thirty years later they find their own children listening to Christian Metal and Christian rap—at least until these kids find secular Metal and Rap more enchanting and better developed. Each person sets his own trajectory in life, and then employs various cultural vehicles to take him there.

4: Christian Kitsch
The Painter of Lite

On April 6, 2012, the most popular "Christian" painter of the 21st century died of "acute intoxication from alcohol and Valium" according to NBC news.[1] His girlfriend of 18 months informed the news media that he had been "drinking all night."[2] At the time, he was still married to a different woman, although they had been separated for two years prior to his death. This artist, Thomas Kinkade, was a self-described "devout Christian" and fashioned himself as the "painter of light."

To understand art, music, and the visual medium, we must first define them by how they are experienced. All three are modes of human expression. They are specialized forms, usually used to affirm the deepest commitments of the human heart. Naturally, there are some commitments that are more profound than others, and it is possible that people will engage in several different types of artistic expression—some representing deeper commitments than others. For example, when a man marries a woman, he commits to a relationship by covenant vows. Throughout the ensuing years, he continues to affirm that relationship by hugs, kisses, and other means of intimate expression. Similarly, while artistic expressions do not establish our basic worldview, values, and commitments, they are effective at confirming them and solidifying our emotional commitment to them.

A few years ago, my wife and I watched the film, *The Notebook* (2004). It was hard not to tear up as an old man cared for his wife who was struggling with Alzheimer's disease. At the end of the story, the two of them died together in each other's arms. Nonetheless, their love story centered on their fornicating relationship and their dishonoring of the young woman's parents. As this story unfolded, I wondered what it was that had secured an emotional commitment from us. Was it possible to separate the immoral elements, which were presented in a good light, from the rest of the love story? Were we separating the good from the bad, even while we appreciated and sympathized with the protagonists in the story? Powerful, dramatic stories like these made into motion pictures, seal a commitment in the minds of the viewers; however, the viewers are often unaware of the nature of that commitment. A few years ago, a hugely popular documentary called *Super Size Me* created a stir against the McDonald's fast food chain. The film followed the lead character as he ate exclusively at the McDonald's fast food chain over the period of one month. Doctors monitored his physical conditions as his health deteriorated and he gained undesired poundage. No doubt, most of those who viewed the documentary could not easily forget the vomit scenes and the poor health of the man as the month progressed, painful day after painful day. Naturally, the presentation would have produced a lasting, emotional frame of mind in most of those who watched it, enough to have affected their eagerness to frequent the fast food establishment. These mediums really do influence the attitudes and behaviors of the viewers, but first, the art form seals the commitment.

Postmodern films ease the listener into a comfortable acceptance of ethical relativism. When the openly homosexual Truman Capote, in the film by the same name, comes to a strange understanding or acceptance of ax murderers, such awful stories will shed new light on Dostoyevsky's words, "If God doesn't exist, everything is permissible." Must we embrace all homosexuals and serial killers as endearing and harmless? Or, should we laud them as brave pioneers who explore the outer frontiers of human ethical autonomy? The film *Truman Capote* landed an Academy Award in 2005. Then, the nihilistic, blood-drenched film, *No Country for Old Men*, dominated the 2007 Academy Award ceremonies. Are we relieved when the existentialist Carly Jean in the story stops a serial killer by challenging him to make the choice himself, instead of flipping a coin to determine the fate of the victim? If postmodern men are finally settling for total ethical relativism and even nihilism, they are revealing their commitment to ultimate hopelessness and chaos in these award-winning films.

THE PAINTER OF LITE

For generations, Christians have been criticized for their lack of depth and originality in their art and music. Years ago, Franky Schaeffer condemned Christian art for what he called an "addiction to mediocrity."[3] But few have really identified the core problems with the expression of this faith in the Western world. If we can identify the core problems, then perhaps we can at least understand why Christians are hardly relevant in the marketplace of ideas (especially in modern, Western, cultural expression). Why does the famous "Christian" artist paint Village Christmas in the morning and die in a drunken stupor in the afternoon? It must be that the Christian is not conscious of his own worldview of resurrection life, of judgment, and righteousness. He must be living on multiple planes. He sits on the fence. He is attempting to bring about cultural expression while he is in the process of apostasy. He may lend some lip service, some external allegiance, to a Jesus-like persona. But at heart, his worldview is more influenced by Carly Jean in *No Country for Old Men* and by Truman Capote.

Many Christians were thrilled to purchase the Debbie Boone hit album *You Light Up My Life* in 1977. The title song was the most popular hit of the 1970s. Although a professing Christian, Boone's contribution to the sexual revolution via the popular music genre was unprecedented. Practically everybody in the 70s was asking the question, "How can it be wrong, if it feels so right?" This was the ethic of the age, and the song spoke to the zeitgeist. It was fitting that songwriter Joe Brooks lived out the ethic and died of suicide in 2011 as he faced 91 charges of rape, sexual assault, etc.[4] Apparently, the courts still considered something wrong even though it felt so right.

My hope is that the reader will gain added discernment from these real-life examples of the cheap facáde of American spirituality and pseudo-Christianity. Much of Christian art is mediocre because the faith has become mediocre, and because Christians do not hold consistently to a Christian worldview. At heart, their epistemology, metaphysic, and ethic are set by the secular humanist worldview; yet they are still clinging to some external semblance of Christianity. For one thing, the churches they attend provide them little solid biblical worldview. Many evangelical churches insist that they are preaching the "gospel," but more and more it is a gospel that is gutted of an authentic biblical worldview. Meanwhile, the world has impressed upon them a purely materialist worldview, an existentialist ethic, and a relativistic concept of truth. This has been accomplished by 90 hours a week of mass media and secular education that is utterly saturated in a false worldview. That a 20-minute Sunday School lesson can counter the thorough indoctrination that happens in the "Matrix" of modern life is hard to conceive.

Why then, all the insipid, trivial art? It is for the simple reason that Christians are insipid and trivial in faith. Where faith is present there is little depth to the faith, and little reason for the faith. When the story of Noah's ark is pictured by the Christian artist, for example, almost inevitably we will see Noah's cute little family and the cute little animals waving at us as they float off into the sunset. What we do not see are the dead, bloated bodies of 500 million men, women, children, and billions of animals drowning in the waters about the ark. Without this more complete picture, there is no meaningful story. We need to know that God was fed up with the evil on the earth, and that He said, "I will kill all flesh from off the earth" (Gen. 6:17, 7:4). In the story of Noah, salvation is set before the backdrop of judgment.

The fuzzy pictures and shallow sentiments beg the question—*Do Christians take themselves seriously, and does anyone else take them seriously?* The "Jesus People" of the sixties and seventies found the empty *formalism* of the fifties problematic, replacing much of it with an empty *informalism*. They thought that if the cultural forms of Christianity (dress, music, etc.) were less formal, perhaps some authenticity to the faith could be salvaged. As it turned out, informalism was not the opposite of empty formalism. This half-hearted attempt to salvage the faith was just as devoid of authenticity and the fear of God. Authenticity does not come that easily. Donning bright red tennis shoes and a T-shirt that reads "No-Fear" will not bring genuine worship into the church, because worship begins with the fear of God. One wonders if some Christian kid might show up on judgment day still wearing his "No Fear" T-shirt and with a "No Fear" energy drink in hand. The eternal Judge of the world would take due note and ask the fellow, "So... what's with the T-shirt?"

To this day, the church in America continues to struggle with hollow, powerless religion. The highest pornography download rates in America are found in the states of Mississippi and Utah—also the states with the highest church attendance rates (Baptists and Mormons).[5] It seems that church guys in suits are caught molesting children or fornicating with the secretary every other day or so (at least if the news reports are trustworthy). Hypocrisy and superficial religiosity are everywhere; no denomination is exempt. These are traits that mark the apostasy of this country.

At the most fundamental level, the Christian view of reality and truth holds the fear of God as the beginning of knowledge (Prov. 1:7). Describing Mr. Fearing in his famous book, John Bunyan referred to the fear of God as the bass in the orchestra. It provides a bedrock for the rest of human expression. It even trumps the fear of man, the fear of terrorists, and the fear of human governments. When a society and a church have been so drained of the fear of God that mentioning it in a church worship service would be the furthest possible consideration, there is little possibility of any true faith. An authentic faith and fear of God must come by the Spirit, and Spirit-filled preaching. This genuine fear of God will lend more gravitas to worship and music, not less. It will lend more gravitas to life. "By mercy and truth iniquity is purged: and by the fear of the LORD men depart from evil" (Prov. 16:6).

Without true faith there can be no meaningful Christian art either. If the beginning of wisdom is the fear of God, then the beginning of Christian culture is the fear of God. The Christian faith will only be as solid as the foundation of that fear and reverence beneath it. Do we truly believe that a holy God sent His only begotten Son to a cruel cross as an atonement for sin in order that His people may be saved from an eternal hell? If so, then this belief would demand a sobriety and gravitas that is largely missing in modern day Christianity. The stakes are not high enough for the post-modern Christian. He opts for Christ as he would opt for Rocky Road ice cream over an anchovy laden pizza. In the mind of the kid in skinny jeans leading the worship band, there isn't a large enough gap between holiness and sinfulness, truth and error, demons and angels, or heaven and hell.

One has a hard time imagining the scene of David severing Goliath's head from his body in a *Precious Moments* knickknack. How would a kitsch Christian artist portray the scene of the old man Samuel hacking King Agag to pieces? Our religion has become too squishy, because there is little fear of God at the root. Sadness and joy mean nothing if there is no fear of God before our eyes.

Several years ago, I tuned in to the "positive and encouraging" local Christian radio station for a period of several days. I listened for the "fear of God" to show up in either lyric or sentiment. Over a two-day period, there was only one song selection that could have helped to form a strong base for Christian culture: "Awesome God." However, the adjective "awesome" has been so overused and abused in the modern vernacular that the average kid couldn't distinguish between an "awesome" skateboard park and an "awesome" God.

There are many themes found in the Book of Psalms that are generally not found in modern music. These include the fear of God, the righteousness and justice of God, the sovereignty of God, the judgment of God, the evil of sin, spiritual and physical warfare, the arch enemies of the Christian, the destruction of the wicked, the reality of hell, the blessedness of the church, the vicious attacks upon the church, the commandments of God, the dominion of David's Son, and so on. Without the backdrop of these truths, the themes of love, mercy, faith, and salvation become largely meaningless. Take, for example Psalm 5:

"Give ear to my words, O Lord, consider my meditation. Hearken

*unto the voice of my cry, my King, and my God: for unto Thee will
I pray. My voice shalt Thou hear in the morning, O Lord; in the
morning will I direct my prayer unto Thee, and will look up."* (Ps.
5:1-3)

These verses were put to music, word-for-word, by songwriter Bill
Sprouse, and it was a prominent selection in the popular Maranatha
music collection of the 1970s and 1980s. The trouble is, the
songwriter forgot to read the rest of the Psalm. What exactly are the
words that this psalmist wishes to bring to the Lord? What is the
substance of his meditation? We read on in the Psalm,

*"For thou art not a God that hath pleasure in wickedness: neither
shall evil dwell with Thee. The foolish shall not stand in Thy sight:
Thou hatest all workers of iniquity. Thou shalt destroy Them that
speak leasing: the Lord will abhor the bloody and deceitful man."*
(Ps. 5:4-6)

These words would hardly have fit into the song Mr. Sprouse put
to music. No doubt, the praise and worship service would have
come to a screeching halt should the band have appended verses
4-6. These verses just would not fit well into the sentiment of
modern spirituality.

The loss of psalmody in the church is one of the early indicators of
the loss of faith. Historically, the preponderance of evidence points
to a predominant use of psalmody in church worship. Whereas the
Christian church has added hymnody throughout the ages, it was
never at the expense of psalmody until the modern age. The church
fathers, the monasteries, and the Reformed churches centered their
worship music in the Psalms. When singing is mentioned in church
history, psalmody is far and away more commonly mentioned than
hymnody. By the 1960s, the hymnbooks in most evangelical churches
had purged the Psalms and replaced these biblical sentiments with
foreign sentiments and emphases. Theologies were adapted to fit the
new liturgy, especially in evangelicalism. Meanwhile, the Psalms draw
hard and fast distinctions between the righteous and the wicked,
something that is not appreciated in a period of religious syncretism.
Many of the Psalms are presented in battle language, written by a

warrior, and intended for those who are in spiritual conflict. As history tells the story, William Wallace, the Braveheart of Scotland, kept a psalter with him constantly in his struggles against the tyranny of England. At his execution, somebody held the psalter up before him to read as he was disemboweled by his enemies. Our Lord also cried out the Psalms, as His life eked from Him upon the cross. True believers will live and breathe the Psalms.

John Calvin called the Book of Psalms "an anatomy of all parts of the soul."[6] All of the range of human emotions are expressed; the Psalms weave an emotional fabric for the human soul. These inspired lyrics take us by the hand and train us in proper emotion. They lead us to emotional maturity. Thus, if the Bible gives us the right way to think about metaphysics, epistemology, and ethics, then the Psalms set a framework for the sanctified and proper emotional and artistic expression. The rejection of psalmody within the church has resulted in general weakness in Christian artistic expression. Sentimentality has been defined as "loving something more than God does."[7] Furthermore, ill-measured sentiments fail to hate that which God hates in the manner that God hates, and fail to love that which God loves in the manner that God loves. Misplaced sentiments love that which God hates, and hates that which God loves. These are emotions that do not resolve themselves in the manner of the inspired Psalms.

5: Context and Mode Matters

I caught a "Holy Hip-Hop" music video on Youtube the other night. It happened to be one of the best recordings of one of the most accomplished Christian artists in the genre. However, I had a hard time paying attention to the lyrics, because I was distracted by the vocalists who kept grabbing at their crotches for some strange reason. One of the musicians sported a floppy T-shirt bearing the word "DESTROYED" in big block letters. The symbolism kept getting in the way of the lyrics for me. This particular song received at least 2,000,000 downloads, which was pretty impressive since the artists kept mentioning somebody named Jesus Christ repeatedly throughout. I kept thinking, Which Christ? Which Christ? Which Christ?

Take the example of the youth leader who wanted to introduce some new Pop symbol into worship. In modern youth culture, the lifting of one particular finger is interpreted as a rude gesture signifying sexual assault. The symbol is considered supremely offensive in civil society, but the youth consider it "cool" especially at popular music concerts. Being that it was "cool," the youth leader decided to introduce the practice into the praise and worship time. Of course, he felt that he was only "robbing the Egyptians" to borrow this symbol. Why not lift the finger in worship? he argued. After all, God has created all five fingers and called them good, and we have liberty to use any or all of them in worship.

For Christian leaders like this, all symbols, all musical genres, and all human practices are legitimate in worship or in the concert hall. Yet most of my readers, even those who wholeheartedly embrace every form of "musical expression" as *adiophora* ("things indifferent") would hesitate here for a moment. *Would it be honoring to God and to each other to use obscene gestures in a worship service?* If a gesture is so closely associated with dishonoring those who are made in God's image, is it appropriate to employ such a gesture? If a symbol has been used to represent teenage pride, social rebellion, an absence of the fear of God, or virulent hatred and wrath, does this symbol belong in the Christian meeting hall where humility and the fear of God must reign supreme? Symbols have particular meanings, and we are all responsible to know what meanings they communicate to our minds and to the minds of others. Leaders especially must be conscious of the symbolic connections.

Consider another case where a senior pastor calls his music director into the church office on a Monday morning. He informs the director that the message on Sunday will focus on the "fear of God." He wants a special number from the music department for the service. Towards the end of the week, the music director returns to the office flushed with excitement. "I've got just what you want, Pastor Jack!" he said. Then, he proceeded to demonstrate the number he had arranged for the Sunday worship. He cranked up his electric guitar and began swaying back and forth. His long hair bounced this way and that to the rhythm of the number. He jumped on the pastor's desk. He grabbed his crotch. Then he let it all out: "You got to... you got to... got to... got to... got to... rev'rence... rev... rev... rev the old man in the skyyyyyyy!" He screamed it out again and again and again.

The senior pastor stared in disbelief. "That's, uh... not going to work," he said.

"Why not?" asked the musical talent.

"Well, I'm just not sensing the reverence. You're not quite capturing the sentiment that I'm trying to convey in my message about the fear of God," the pastor said.

First we must ask if we have selected the right sentiment to carry the words or ideas. Then, we need to determine whether we have selected the right mode to convey the sentiment. Suppose that a film producer was to adapt a screen play on the David and Bathsheba incident in the Bible. For the most part, he stayed true to Scripture, except he elected to include a steamy Jacuzzi scene complete with writhing nude bodies that netted the movie an R-rating. Even Nathan the prophet wouldn't have been able to compensate for the damage done in that single scene.

Yes, it is possible to ruin a film with a single scene, and a painting can be destroyed by a single paint stroke. Put a black streak across the upper lip of the Mona Lisa, and she has a mustache. Now the painting can't even be sold for $25 at a garage sale. The method or mode chosen for the art form may create internal conflicts within the form and contradictions with the message. This is exactly what the postmodernist has in mind. Indeed, he *expects* the expressed mode to contradict the message. Given that the postmodernist has abandoned the possibility of order and meaning, he requires contradictions everywhere—especially in his religious music. The lyrics are accidental—not of essence. Fundamentally, his worldview is not aligned to the objective truth of Scripture. He is a post-modern relativist. Sure, he may have "given his heart" to Jesus at some point, but he retains his fundamental worldview of relativism. His worldview was determined by the 120,000 hours of indoctrination he received via media and educational institutions. The 20-minute teaching he received on a Sunday morning never quite countered what he picked up from the zeitgeist.

ALL THINGS ARE NOT EXPEDIENT

"All things are lawful for me, but all things are not expedient: all things are lawful for me, but all things edify not." (1 Cor. 10:23)

At this point, I'm sure that I have disappointed a fair percentage of my audience. Some of my readers may have expected me to just come out and say it. Scrawl it out on the cover of the book with a ham-handed grip on the thick crayon, big guy: *"All Rock n' Roll is of the divel!"* Another segment of my audience is wondering why I make such a big deal of popular culture. "Aren't all things lawful? Shouldn't Christian liberty free us to do whatever we want, with the possible exceptions of mass murder and bank robbery?" This is not the gist of the Apostle's point in Colossians 3. Cultural discernment is not that simple. There is need for great wisdom in cultural application. In order to live the Christian life and develop proper cultural forms, we need to screw our brains in place and "love God with our heart, soul, *mind*, and strength" (Deut. 6:4-5).

When Paul says all things are lawful for me, but all things are not expedient, he means that there are certain forms that belong in certain contexts. There is an appropriate time and place for everything. It remains for us to find out what the time and place is for all things, and thereby edify ourselves and our brothers and sisters in Christ. To rightly apply cultural symbols, we must understand the principle of food offered to idols. When food offered to idols is sold in the market, the Christian has no scruples about purchasing the meat for $1.20 a pound (1 Cor. 10:25). But if he happens to be sitting in the temple where the sacrifice is happening, he must refrain from eating the meat so as not to send the message that he participates and condones the idolatry in the minds of the idolators, the demons, or himself (1 Cor. 10:27-29). Thus, symbols retain something of a sacramental significance—depending on the situation and the existential perspective of those involved.

What would my parishioners say if I were to roll into the church parking lot on a Sunday morning, with a Playboy bunny prominently displayed on my rear window? No doubt, some would interpret the symbol as my endorsement of the Playboy philosophy. However, a little African boy may end up getting a T-shirt sporting the Playboy symbol, but for this little boy, it's just a rabbit. It's lunch for him. The context establishes the association between the symbol and that which it symbolizes.

Christians should exercise caution when handling certain brand names, for example. When Abercrombie and Fitch became singularly and widely known for their homoerotic and sexually explicit advertising, many Christians were hesitant to sport this company's trademark on their clothing and accessories. However, when a young

Christian man begins wearing this clothing, what does it mean to him? Of course, he won't normally admit right off the bat that he supports homoeroticism on the first day that he associates himself with this "edgy" clothing company. Yet it's hard to imagine that he doesn't absorb the homoeroticism or the sexual connotations in the seven-foot-high posters plastered on the windows of the stores. *All symbols mean things.* All of us bear some responsibility to discern the symbols within our respective cultures. And, let none of us pretend to be ignorant, as if we never form any associations in our minds, because human beings always make associations. Clearly, the Apostle Paul maintains that every Christian is responsible for discerning these associations wherever they appear. For example, certain hand gestures acceptable in one culture are unacceptable in another and can even be insulting. Missionaries in Japan are careful when visiting a graveyard or participating in tea ceremonies to avoid lending credence to certain religious, idolatrous practices. 1 Corinthians 10:27-29 can be effectively applied in this context.

As the Western world becomes a blend of many religions and worldviews, Christians must be more discerning than ever. Take for example, the use of Yoga and Eastern Medicinal practices. Do Christians immediately adopt every pagan idea and practice, just because their neighbors are doing it? Of course not. Otherwise, Christians would amalgamate into every false religion, and the faith would die out. Japanese Christians would revert back to Shintoism, Saudi Christians to Islam, and Irish Christians would return to Druid life and culture.

Yet, what if there were some alternate "benefit" of a heathen practice, while the ideas that formed the practice were false and idolatrous? For the purposes of our study, we'll consider a make-believe case. Suppose that a "religious guru" taught that human life is tied into an impersonal universal force (or even that we were all part of one universal life force). In his religious musings, he discovered a method by which to heal migraine headaches. To "engage the life force" for its healing capabilities, the guru merely blew through a drinking straw upon the head of the patient. As it turned out, several of his patients were actually healed through the use of this method. These "true" healings may have come about because of a real cause and effect relationship that has yet to be explained by a proper method. Perhaps blowing air through straws onto people's heads really cures migraines. Or, maybe a supernatural, counterfeit demonic power has entered the scene a time or two and effected a cure. Or it may have been a case of psychosomatic reaction, or the patient may have faked his response to the treatment.

Whatever the case, the Christian must first analyze the ideas taught by the "religious guru" who concocted the weird practice. If the doctrines taught relating to the nature of the universe, the nature of God, or the nature of man is incompatible with Scripture, the doctrines themselves must be rejected out of hand. As far as the practices are concerned, there is nothing inherently sinful about blowing air through a straw against the foreheads of others. But, as long as such a practice is connected to false ideas, it ought to be rejected by the Christian. He should lend no credence to false teachings. He should be careful not to recommend the man's websites, brochures, books, and literature. However, he may test the practice independently, and develop his own theory as to the cause and effect relationship. There is nothing sinful about recommending the practice to others, if he is willing to take the time and expense to conduct a public, well documented, scientific study on the practice, and subject himself to peer review. If, however, the effectiveness of the practice has never been tested, and the proponents resist testing, the Christian must conclude that there is dishonesty and subterfuge involved in the practice. All things are lawful, but not all things are helpful to cure migraines.

THE SOCIAL CONTEXT

Cultural symbols often embody an entire social and cultural experience. Thus, those who embrace the symbols find that they affirm and confirm their own social experience. In fact, culture will root itself in the social context. There would have been no cultural revolutions, had there not been social revolutions. This is what happened in the creation of modern music. For example, the honky tonk sound was formed in the honky tonk bar, and loose life was characterized by the bar scene. Johnny Horton set his hit song "Honky Tonk Man," in the context of a bar, where he bought the drinks, danced with the girls, and phoned his wife at home when he ran out of money. Some men who enjoyed the honky tonk sound lived the honky tonk life. Others did not—and only wished they could.

Pop music was formed largely for the benefit of the youth. There would have been no Frank Sinatra, no Elvis Presley, no Beatles, no Rolling Stones, no KISS, no Michael Jackson, no Madonna, no Kurt Cobain, no Lady Gaga, and no Eminem if there had been no youth. Without the development of a youth peer culture and large junior high and high schools, there would have been none of the Pop culture we see now. For thousands of years, parents and local pastors formed the culture. Entertainment happened around the fireplace during long winter nights when Pa played the fiddle and the children danced around the living room together. Folk stories and Folk wisdom passed from grandparent to parent to child, generation by generation. All of that is gone now, as the social revolutions of the 19th and 20th centuries fragmented the family, destroyed family economies, and produced a new "youth culture."

Over the last twenty years, my wife and I chose to raise our children in a different social context. We emphasized family over a peer social setting. We built a family economy, and all of our children participated along the way. Our children never attended conventional schools, and never preferred the peer group to the family. Their friends were anywhere from ten years younger to forty years older. We watched movies together, and we took vacations together. Consequently, our children do not relate to Neil Sedaka's hit song "Breaking Up Is Hard to Do" (#1 in 1962, and #8 in 1975 on the Pop charts), or a thousand other popular songs that express the same basic idea. These do not make the "Top 40" in our home. If our children were attending a typical high school, of course they would have related to this break-up-and-make-up song. The only scenario in which a song like this would sell twenty million copies is the setting in which hosts of young people are participating in the dating culture. Of course, this culture did not exist prior to the 1920s. Pop stars like Neil

Sedaka and Pop hits like "Breaking Up Is Hard to Do" were cultural icons or symbols made to order for the teenage social setting of the 1950s, 1960s, and 1970s. As the social habits shifted from dating and break ups in the 1960s, to shack ups in the 1980s, and then to hook ups in the 2000s, the music had to change in turn. Given that teenagers now are more interested in lesbianism, sadomasochism, and sexual nihilism than they are in Neil Sedaka, it makes sense that Pop star Miley Cyrus speaks of promiscuity with "whomever" in her chart topper, "We Can't Stop." Katy Perry encourages young women to lesbianism in her "I Kissed a Girl," and other Pop artists encourage their teenage listeners to rape and sadism. Thus, we will continue to see the message and form change radically every ten years or so to accommodate the social context. It is hard to know how long this cultural revolution will last.

If the battle for social context is raging anywhere, you will see it in Country music—where there really appears to be a struggle going on between the blue cities and the red rural communities. There is a tug-of-war between the metro-sexual, urban cowboy and the man who honors the seventh commandment and loves his wife "forever and ever, Amen." The song "Detroit City" clarified this social tension when Bobby Bare took the song to #6 on the Country charts in 1963. The song is set in Detroit, Michigan, where the protagonist makes the cars by day and he makes the bars by night. Deep down, he still wants to return home to momma and papa, and the girl who has been waiting to marry him. The family social setting is still important, but it appears to be fading in the glare of the city lights, and the anonymous life of the vagabond in the big city.

If we were to do a quick survey of the top ten Country songs in 2013, we would still find a song about a man who wants to repent of his cheating and get right with his wife. But eight out of ten songs deal with checking out a girl for a temporary sexual hook up, living together out of wedlock, and divorce as a social norm. From my observations, the Pop culture fare stays slightly ahead of the populace in its efforts to break moral and social norms. Popular media is always a bit more edgy than the people who consume it. Nonetheless, the people that receive those cultural expressions that embody broken social and moral conditions will soon pattern these conditions in their own lives.

CULTURAL SYMBOLS

All that said, we don't want to oversimplify the matter. The fact remains that cultures are complex. In the Western world especially, there is an intricate weave that comprises our cultural heritage. This includes remnants from ancient pagan cultures, Christian practices from the previous millennium, as well as false ideas and practices taken on since the great apostasy commenced in the 18th century. Various tribal traditions from other nationalities have made their way into the American cultural mix. Meanwhile, outside of the Western world, there are various people groups, including recent immigrants, who are turning to Christ and setting new cultural trajectories all the time. Hence, every pastor and spiritual leader must take care to establish Christian strands of culture wherever they have influence. They must also be careful not to condemn cultural expressions from other cultures until they understand the heart of the people group. Good questions to ask when assessing any new cultural expression are: What is their fundamental worldview? Are they changing hearts and minds by the preaching of the Word of God? Is this already in process? How does their cultural expression connect to their fundamental worldview commitment?

As we analyze our own culture, we must use a thin-bladed scalpel to cut between that which has Christian connotations and that which bears anti-Christian connotations. A missionary to the South Seas in the 19th century would have an easy time pointing out the ungodly cultural systems he encountered, simply because those tribes had no Christian heritage at all. Where pagan cultures do retain some common grace, where they respect human life, honor their parents and grandparents, and preserve the sanctity of marriage, they ought to be recognized for it. The inner-city African American culture likely constitutes a blend of ancient paganism in addition to Christian roots lodged in their old simple Folk spirituals, together with the influence of the modern welfare state, socialism, and humanism rooted in Western apostasy.

In the critique of cultures, we ought also to be on guard against hypocrisy and judgmentalism (condemned by Christ in Matt. 7:1-4). It is proper to judge, but to judge by a standard to which we would never hold ourselves is patently wrong. Nonetheless, we must believe that God's Word sets an adequate standard whereby we may judge the relative magnitude of evil in cultures. For example, the homosexuality and adultery that characterize much of the rotting Christian church in the Western world indicate that the world is in a worse condition than the pagan nations that practice polygamy. According to biblical law (and New Testament reference), polygamy is not treated as a capital crime. An apostate Western world thinks of itself as having achieved the ultimate heights of moral superiority, but fails to submit itself to the standards of God's law. A little humility is in order here—if the old, white Protestants are in apostasy, they are hardly in a position to judge those pagan tribes which are repenting of sin and transforming their cultures by the grace of Christ.

6: The Tattooed Jesus

Universal Symbolic Forms

"It seemed good to the Holy Spirit and to us, to lay upon you no greater burden than these necessary things: that you abstain from things offered to idols, from blood, from things strangled, and from sexual immorality. If you keep yourselves from these, you do well." (Acts 15:28-29)

The Word of God does not leave us without a standard for human culture. The truths contained in biblical revelation apply cross-culturally, and they give us an ethical standard for all times and places. Within these biblical standards, diverse cultures may develop, and God's law will provide for maximum cultural diversity and maximum unity, while establishing for the best and most precise standard of God's righteousness. But the question still remains, how do we best apply the law of God? Paul condemns those who use the law unlawfully in 1 Timothy 1:8-11. From my perspective, the safest approach to handling the law is to teach it and apply it as the Apostles and Christ did in Scripture.

Acts 15:28-29 summarizes the final decisions issued by the first New Testament church council, and it drew on Old Testament teaching and practice. The question before the elders was whether to require that the Gentiles be circumcised according to Old Testament law (Ex. 12:48), or whether they should dispense with the Old Testament law entirely. The question of circumcision related to a ceremonial external that distinguished the Old Testament Jews from the surrounding nations. The Apostles concluded that the practice was no longer necessary for the people of God. However, they refused to throw out the entire Old Testament law. Instead, they retained several law categories in their instructions to the New Testament churches. First, the moral laws relating to sexual immorality (the 7th commandment) were to be upheld. Secondly, the law relating to the consumption of blood was retained (Lev. 17:14, 19:26.) which was a law category referring to certain universal symbols that apply across all cultures and all periods of human history. The third prohibition was related to the subject of food offered to idols, which we take as temporary symbols and sacraments that apply at specific times and situations, as Paul further develops in 1 Corinthians 10.

The New Testament writers did not spend a great deal of time clarifying the application of Old Testament law. Yet, the Apostles felt it was necessary to underscore the importance of these moral imperatives.

The first Christian martyrs faced with charges of cannibalism and incest (and other sexual sins), told their accusers that these were "crimes as are neither lawful for us to speak nor to think."[1] Moreover, the martyr Biblias argued her case by asking the simple question, "How could such as these devour children, who consider it unlawful even to taste the blood of irrational animals?" This courageous Christian woman was only upholding the apostolic declaration against the consumption of blood contained in Acts 15, and the clear commandment of Old Testament law (Lev. 17:10-14).[2]

Have you ever wondered why most apostate nations are fixated on the consumption of blood? Why are vampire movies among the most popular of our day? Why does almost half of the twenty-something population sport tattoos? Why were the European, Western missionaries working diligently in the 19th century to remove tattoos and obliterate polygamy and cannibalism, if now their grandchildren and great-grandchildren are enthusiastically embracing vampirism, tattoos, body mutilation, adrogeny, and other pagan practices by the millions? Perhaps it is because these are the universal symbols of paganism.

The consumption of the placenta or after-birth is yet another pagan practice that is soundly condemned as definitively evil in

Deuteronomy 28:57. However, the practice has become increasingly popular among "Christians" in the early part of the 21st century. Pagans have always understood the blood-rich organs to provide health and strength, and these customs have been revived lately. These universal pagan principles die hard.

Leviticus 19 lists a number of these universal symbols of paganism. It isn't always easy to identify the things that they symbolize. However, the consumption of blood must stand for the desecration of life, because Leviticus 17:10-14 plainly tells us that "the life is the blood." Other universal symbols of paganism include:

The practice of divination or soothsaying (Lev. 19:26).

Shaving the sides of the beard—removing all signs of masculinity that were placed there by God (Lev. 19:27).

Making cuttings on your flesh for the dead (Lev. 19:28).

Tattoo marks on the body (Lev. 19:28).

Prostitution of daughters (Lev. 19:29).

The tattoo is virtually omnipresent today in Western countries—especially America. Movie stars, sports figures, models, and Miss America contestants decorate their bodies with these markings. According to Pew Research, 38% of young people (18-29 years old) are tattooed.[3] Only 5% of adults over 64 years of age are tattooed, many of whom have recently obtained these flesh markings.[4] There is an unmistakable comparison between these postmodern pagans and the pagan tribes in the jungles of Africa and South America that were discovered by Christian explorers after thousands of years of demonic dominion. The patterns of the heathen do seem to validate the Old Testament laws addressing universal pagan symbols. While the sacrificial laws, sabbaths, circumcision, and food laws were specifically changed by clear New Testament revelation, the Apostles went out of their way to validate these Old Testament laws relating to pagan symbols. It is not always clear *why* the pagans want to eliminate gender distinctions in clothing, hair, and appearance, or why they get a thrill out of vampirism and cannibalism, or why they tattoo their bodies, or why they boil a young goat in its mother's milk (Deut. 14:21). The psychological explanation for such symbolic actions are not always clear, but the practices seem to crop up repeatedly among pagan tribes. During World War II, some of the Japanese military leaders revived the practice of cannibalism, still asserting that life and strength may be derived from the blood-rich organs such as the human liver.[5] Some symbols are universal–old habits die hard.

Perhaps at this point, we should answer our original question. *Would Jesus tattoo Leviticus 19:28 on His left thigh?* The answer is clearly "No. He wouldn't." The simple answer to the question, "What would Jesus do?" is very simply, "The will of God." Jesus would obey His Father's will as expressed in Scripture. He would not commit adultery. He would not murder. He would not eat blood. He would honor His parents. He would not tattoo Leviticus 19:28 on His left thigh.

Whether the cultural rite is local or universal, the Christian must inquire as to what these symbols express. Sometimes the meaning is obvious. Sometimes the meaning is interpreted for us by God's Word (in the universal symbols). Nose and ear piercing express clearly the idea of bondage or submission. Thus, the Bible allows piercing for males in the Old Testament only when they submit themselves to permanent servitude (Ex. 21:4-6).

Pagan culture will readily acknowledge that body mutilation symbolizes bondage and sado-masochism. It is only the Christians (or people who still want to be perceived as decent Folk), who dabble in extreme body mutilation that will lie to themselves for a little while concerning what these things really mean. It may take a few months or even a few years before they "come out of the closet," and admit to their apostasy. Inevitably, self-consistency of type and antitype (or symbol and thing symbolized) will surface. Still, we must always allow room for a change of mind or a change of worldview. When the Gospel of Christ penetrates, lives are transformed by the renewing of minds. And, it is the renewal of minds that results in renewal of culture.

This is no minor issue. Christians had better figure this stuff out.

When they tattoo and body pierce the body of Christ (or professing Christians), are they expressing false ideas and the wrong faith? Are they piercing the body of the wrong Christ? Have they morphed the real Christ into a horrible semblance of some pagan god? As we encounter the pantheon of modern Christian apostasies, cults, and counterfeits, the faithful are crying out, "Will the real Christ please stand up!"

Most often, people will speak of tattoos as an "expression of my individuality." They take pictures of their tattoos, and write on their Facebook accounts, "This is the way that I want to define myself." By taking the body that God has given them, and permanently changing it by an individual act of the will, men and women feel that they are self-defining and self-creating. While these ideas are warmly accepted by the postmodern humanists, they run exactly counter to the biblical faith. The devil offered self-determination for Eve, and she accepted it. This is what constituted the original sin. It is only gods that self-determine by an act of "sovereign" will. A quick survey of tattooing sites, will find this interpretation of the tattoo is practically universal. Man wants to self-define. For the Christian however, there is no ultimate self-definition. God creates us and He providentially orders our lives. He gives meaning to our lives, and He tells us what to think about our lives. God tells us what to do with our lives. We belong to the heavenly Master, our Creator. We are not our own. We are bought with a price. Glorify God in your body which is God's (1 Cor. 6:19-20).

Tattooing is also a rite that identifies a man with his tribe, his girlfriend, or with "Jesus." Christians have identified themselves with Christ by way of a sacrament called "baptism," a mark that burns deep into the soul. It is the ultimate "tattoo," cutting as deep as circumcision. This identification with Christ in baptism was so deep that some believers viewed it as a form of unification with Christ (Rom. 6:3). Some wrongly equated it to regeneration, but most Christians took it as an important seal or bond. Through the years, the sacrament of baptism has become increasingly unimportant, even irrelevant to the modern Christian. As faith has dissipated, some have found new commitments, and with their new commitments they find new sacraments by which they identify themselves. Hoping to commit themselves to Christ, they identify themselves with this Christ by tattooing a gigantic cross on their chest, or the word "Jesus" across their forehead. With the decline of the one sacrament, came the rise of a new rite. What does Christ think about this? What would the great men of faith like Patrick of Ireland, John Paton, John Calvin, and Martin Luther think of it?

When pagans become Christians, they take on a new commitment, which is sealed by baptism. Their old commitments and their old tattoos no longer matter. What does matter now is their relationship with Christ, sealed by their baptism. They do not need another "christ," and they do not need any other sacraments. After committing adultery with other women, an unfaithful husband comes to his senses and returns to his wife. He sees the value of his original commitment—sealed by the original vows and the ring. When he puts that ring back on his finger, he feels the significance of it to the depths of his being. He repents of his adulterous apostasy, and settles into a lifetime of faithfulness to his one and only love. This is the counsel to be provided those believers who are delivered from the paganism of the modern form.

How do Christian parents react when their son comes home from college sporting tattoos and various body piercings and mutilations? As with all cultural expressions, the parent is concerned with the true worldview behind the expression. What is the trajectory of the heart? What does this young man truly believe about God, about himself, and about redemption? Do the accoutrements of bondage indicate a true love for bondage (Ex. 21:5-6)? Has the Son really set us free from the bondage of sin and guilt (John 8:34-36)? Why is this yet to be fully apprehended? Do the vain attempts to self-atone, indicate a rejection of the only effectual atonement—Christ's death on the cross?

For parents, these are opportunities for self-reflection. Sometimes, the sons will express with more honesty the true heart commitments of the father. Has faith faded from generation to generation, as it did in the legacy of Clarence and Ernest Hemingway?

So far there is nothing to say about piercings and tattoos. The conversation turns towards substantial matters - the Red Sea deliverance and Calvary. What is it about the bondage of Egypt and sin that is more attractive than Christ? What associations are more powerful than our association with Christ, and why? What is to be found in these ineffectual associations? Why is there so little faith or interest in water baptism and the thing for which it signifies? Thus, the thoughtful parent is not first concerned with outward appearances. He is concerned with the heart. He is concerned with himself. He is concerned with eternity.

7: The Cultural Command
Honor Your Father and Mother

Occasionally, some young person will ask me what I think about Contemporary Christian Music, or what I think about Rock n' Roll music. "Should I listen to it?" they ask. My comeback typically is, "What do your parents think about it?" This is a valid question, assuming that the fifth commandment holds relevance to life and culture. The fifth commandment is tied to a promise, and that promise addresses the blessing that God brings to culture in a community (Ex. 20:12, Eph. 6:1-2).

Given that the social context is critical to the development of culture and music specifically, it is helpful to know that the Pop star Eminem is the son of a single mother. This is not unusual in that many modern musicians are products of broken families, to include John Lennon of Beatles fame. Marshall Mathers (pseudonym Eminem) made a career out of breaking the fifth commandment, selling over 115 million albums and netting himself the title, "King of Hip-Hop." It would be difficult to identify any other cultural icon in the history of the world (in pagan or Christian nation), that gained such popular ascendance on the grossest possible violations of the fifth commandment. He referred to his mother as a female dog and worse.[1] Such brave blasphemous irreverence captured the hearts and minds of a generation whose teeth were like knives. While these Pop stars may be bastards in the traditional sense of the word, and their mothers immoral women, these tirades constitute the most vile reference possible towards the woman who gave him life. This lack of honor only perpetuates the curse of God upon successive generations. Most tragic of all is the reception of such social corruption and cultural disintegration on the part of hundreds of millions of young people. Marshall Mathers spoke to the heart of youth in revolt against God and His social order. Johann Sebastian Bach and Isaac Watts produced the culture of the 18th century. The shift to "Rape Rap" in the 20th century has been radical and severe.

Cultures fall hard and fast when successive generations revolt against each previous generation. This is also a recipe for societal collapse. When the rappers speak of mothers as female dogs, and make regular positive and negative reference to the rape of parents, one cannot help but think of Proverbs 30:11-14:

> "There is a generation that curseth their father, and doth not bless their mother. There is a generation that are pure in their own eyes, and yet is not washed from their filthiness. There is a generation, O how lofty are their eyes! And their eyelids are lifted up. There is a generation, whose teeth are as swords, and their jaw teeth as knives, to devour the poor from off the earth, and the needy from among men."

Assaults on the fundamental social order often serve as a precursor to dangerous and bloody revolutions. If this passage has never applied to any culture over the past 4000 years, the last forty years and four hundred million music albums well represent "the generation that curses their father and does not bless their mother." Although our nations have not yet witnessed much blood in the streets, real or figurative patricide is its predecessor. The Book of Proverbs also offers a proper cultural vision for the young man who honors his father and mother.

> "My son, hear the instruction of your father, and do not forsake the law of your mother, for they will be a graceful ornament on your head and chains about your neck." (Prov. 1:8-9)

> "My son, forget not my law; but let thine heart keep my commandments: For length of days, and long life, and peace, shall they add to thee." (Prov. 3:1-2)

Granted, references to "law of your mother" or "commandments of your father" is puzzling when the Old Testament saints are committed to the law of God (Eccl. 12:13). If however, the parent's instructions and laws are understood to be the cultural applications of the commandments of God, then the references make sense. When a family attempts to live out reverence for God, love for neighbor, and honor of parents, they will do so through a variety of day-to-day applications. Every family will express fear, love, and honor in different ways, and they will train their children in these ways. This is typically where manners come from. Should a mother teach her son to make his bed, tuck in his shirt, and say "Yes Ma'am," she is only teaching the boy to live out honor and love for others. Of course, there is the occasional boy who plays the lawyer, pointing out that Jesus never tucked in his shirt, and there's nothing about this "Yes Ma'am" business or making beds in Scripture. "Isn't Mom imposing extra-biblical laws upon her son here?" Actually, Mom is doing her best to apply God's principles in the context of her family. The fifth commandment expects a son to honor these laws, and never to forsake the law of his mother. As the young man grows up and leaves the home, the expectation is that he will continue to honor the heritage and training received from his mother. As he binds these things around his heart and hands, he will find new and better ways to express reverence, love, and honor. Everything he has learned from his parents concerning manners, dress, music, theology, organization, conversation, exercise, eating, and devotion become the starting point for his life. As he honors his heritage, he stands upon the shoulders of previous generations. He builds upon this heritage, taking it farther and deeper. This is how culture is enriched and preserved. This is how things "go well for us in the land." When a son honors whatever good heritage he receives from his father or his mother, he stands on their shoulders and culture advances. Although some children bemoan a poor heritage they have received from dysfunctional parents, there may still be something to honor in the family legacy. Standing on the shoulders of parents who lie flat on their backs will put the son or daughter six inches off the ground.

A wise expression of honor will necessarily recognize wisdom on the part of the parent. For example, a father who recommends a drug habit for his son, or presses his son into drunkenness offers him no wisdom. A wise son therefore, will reject wicked counsel and a bad cultural trajectory. By overlooking and avoiding his father's unwise and bad behavior (as in the case of Noah's drunkenness), the son expresses honor for his father as best as he can.

On the other hand, if parents provide even a modicum of wisdom in life, whether it be in the area of eating habits, music, entertainment, clothing, or manners, a wise son will receive it and benefit culturally. Generally speaking, parents will retain a better compendium of life wisdom than Lady Gaga and Elvis Presley (and the other Pop culture heroes).

RESPECTING THE FAMILY JURISDICTION

At least for Christians, the individual must still remember that he is a member of a covenant community (family and/or church). His cultural choices have some influence on the other members of his community, although more so in family than church. Thus, he is responsible not only for himself, but also for the rest of the covenant body. This recognition may press the individual back into isolation as the modern existentialist who wishes that nobody impinge upon his moral and cultural choices.

Biblically, a Christian brother must be willing to deny himself if he will offend the weaker brother, if his brother is grieved with him, or would be weakened by his example (Rom. 14:15). While he watches his films and updates his Facebook account, he must remember that his actions may bear upon others in his local church. Also, the young woman must be sensitive to the brothers in the church, who may be easily offended by her immodest dress.

Nonetheless, the family jurisdiction should enjoy maximum liberty, and the church must be careful not to tread on these liberties (Rom. 14:1-5). Movies, music, manners, and clothing choices are first set by families who live in covenant with each other. Above all, fathers must understand the spiritual needs of their households, avoiding all offense to "the least of these who believe" in Christ (Matt. 18:6). Individual families will generally maintain a strongly uniform interpretation of their cultural symbols, especially where fathers are loving leaders and children honor their fathers and mothers.

YOU SAY YOU WANT A REVOLUTION

It would be impossible to correctly read the times without fully realizing the impact of revolutionary thought upon the modern world. These are the days of upheaval. Few historians would argue this point. Certainly, political revolutions have been commonplace, but it is the social and cultural revolutions that have taken the most ground in the old Christian world. Eminem's rape Rap would never have appealed to 19th century Americans. They were singing "My grandfather's clock was too large for the shelf, so it stood ninety years on the floor." This was the age of families, parents and grandparents. There would have been no Eminem or John Lennon had there not been broken families. Social revolutions produce cultural revolutions.

For over one hundred years, the phenomenon was growing in gestational form. But the thing was born on October 12, 1944, when 30,000 frenzied, teeny-bopping girls descended upon Times Square to meet their new idol—Frank Sinatra! Writer Bruce Bliven described the scene as "a phenomenon of mass hysteria that is only seen two or three times in history." It was the teenager. In his book, *Teenage: The Creation of Youth Culture*, social commentator Jon Savage chronicles this remarkable facet of modern culture, practically a paradigmatic anomaly unparalleled in prior human history.[2]

In retrospect, it seems that this was a "necessary" element of life for the new industrialized, mass-populated modern city. Anonymity and transient relationships became the norm. Men like J.M. Barrie and Oscar Wilde glorified the image of eternal youth, and the life of leisure inevitably became the highest value to every developing empire. Attending this new cultural milieu was the obligatory dishonoring of parents, generational severance, family disintegration, child labor laws, family-fragmenting corporations, public schools, sexual assertion on the part of girls, Pop culture icons, immodesty, dating, and teen fornication. The connections in this social and cultural grid are inextricably linked. I doubt that Almanzo Wilder's sisters would have ever shown up at New York Times Square in 1875 to meet some popular teen heart throb like Frank Sinatra. Without 70 years of age-segregated, public school education between 1875 and 1944, Frank Sinatra would never have mesmerized 30,000 screaming female fans in Times Square on October 12th, 1944.

For hundreds of years, even thousands of years, churches were filled with a healthy cross-section of children, parents, and grandparents. They would sing the same songs, with slight modifications generation by generation. There were no separately designated "traditional" services and "contemporary" services. Worship was cross-generational, and culture transferred seamlessly from generation to generation.

While there are comparatively few differences to be found in church music between 1550 and 1960, monumental shifts occurred after 1960. Perhaps more importantly however, the cultural connections between the Maranatha music of the 1970s, the Vineyard songs of the 1980s, and the Wonder Jam standards of the 2010s are tenuous or nonexistent. With very few exceptions, the Silent Generation is not jamming to Wonder Jam. Grandparents and grandchildren generally do not attend the same churches. If they do, chances are the worship music is still the "old stuff." Teenagers yawn through the service, and crank up their iPods as quickly as possible after the service to catch the latest in contemporary sounds. Within a few years, they will be attending different churches, if they attend any church at all. To compensate, churches rushed out to offer different worship services for the elderly, the Gen Xers, and the Millennials.

How do churches survive without cultural connections between the generations? How will society survive? What will this revolution produce? If fruitful cultural expression is a matter of wisdom or a wise application of worldview, what happens when there is little or no cultural connection with the previous generation? The breakdown of the cross-generational church turns into the breakdown of the church. Without older women mentoring the younger women, and older men teaching the younger men (Titus 2:1-8), where will the church be in the year 2060?

To understand modern culture, we must understand the concept of "the cool." Sociologists define "cool" as a socially "admired aesthetic, attitude, behavior, comportment, appearance and style, influenced by and a product of the zeitgeist."[3] The cool person seeks a certain "strategic social value with the peer context."[4] "Cool" became the language of revolution in the 1960s, where the revolutionary would avoid outright rebellion to governing authorities, but hide "defiance behind a wall of ironic detachment."[5]

If "cool" is a fundamental disposition and value that frames the attitude and behavior of the youth, the Christian wants to know how it competes with the fear of God and honor of parents. Does "cool" still allow for the fear of God as the controlling predisposition? Recently, I received a church magazine sporting a front-cover feature photo of a young man with a baseball cap cocked on his bowed head. The theme of the magazine was prayer. Setting 1 Corinthians 11:4[6] aside, I wondered if the magazine editor took into account the cultural milieu and the disposition implied by the comportment of the man in the picture. What would Augustine or Paul think of this magazine cover? Of course, "cool" is not a biblical value, and as far as it competes with the fear of God, it is to be rejected. Does "cool" maintain Christian humility and the fear of God? Can "cool" adequately present human dignity (as man created in the image of God, a little lower than the angels), or is "cool" rooted in human pride? If the fear of God is the beginning of wisdom (i.e. it's important), and if it is of any relevance in the Christian life, we need to ask these questions from time to time. Fear and "cool" are not necessarily mutually exclusive. Nonetheless, it would be refreshing to see Christians who pay more attention to faithfully adhere to the commandments of God, in reference to culture. Too frequently, Christians wish to turn every cultural expression into a matter of *adiophora* (things indifferent), not realizing that culture is the central battleground for worldviews.

ROLE MODELS

Closely tied to the idea of "cool" are role models. Many young teens will identify with sports stars, popular music performers, and movie stars, with the desire to emulate them. They find something cool in the leering look made popular by Elvis Presley and James Dean, or the twerking of Miley Cyrus and the ubiquitous mockery of Lady Gaga. Accordingly, they will form their attitudes, dress, hairstyles, lifestyle, morals, and life goals around these popular stars. Not for a moment do they think about the worthwhile accomplishments and true character of these celluloid stars. They toss a ball around an indoor court and drop it through a net. Some of them can even pretend to be courageous and shoot fake guns at fake enemies. Most of them are proven at fornication and divorce, and the ruination of their families. Young people are quicker to idolize drunks like Mel Gibson (internationally acclaimed actor) and adulterers like Tiger Woods (world champion golfer), than they would appreciate a story about Polycarp or Athanasius. How many Christian families provided posters of Hannah Montana for their daughter's bedrooms, despite alter-ego Miley Cyrus' record of playing with fornication and drugs along the way? Why wouldn't they have preferred pictures of the martyr Blandina or Perpetua who gave up their lives for Christ in the bloody coliseum? Our role models, the people we admire most, reveal the true inclinations of the heart.

HIGH ART, FOLK ART, AND POP ART

Kenneth A. Myers helpfully distinguishes three categories of art in his book *All God's Children and Blue Suede Shoes*. He defines Pop art as popular, transient, expendable (easily forgotten), low-cost, mass-produced, young, witty, gimmicky, and often sexy and glamorous.[7]

How many remember singing the choruses "Thy Loving Kindness Is Better than Life" or, "Lord I Lift Your Name on High?" These are examples of Christian "Pop art" from the 1970s. Church congregations have been singing "Oh Sacred Head Now Wounded" for 800 years—that is anything but transient, expendable, and gimmicky. It is doubtful that Maranatha songs from the 1970s are going to be anything but an occasional nostalgic golden oldie in another few years. Low cost. Mass-produced. Gimmicky. Expendable.

Myers describes traditional (Folk) culture and high culture as focusing on the timeless, encouraging reflection, emphasizing wisdom, celebrating ability vs. fame, honoring the past, requiring a submission to standards, and having enduring qualities.

The difference between Folk culture and high culture, as I see it, is only a matter of generations. High culture honors forty generations, and Folk culture honors four generations. The popular culture model honors transient fame and praises whomever happens to come up with the best gimmick at the right moment. Pop culture is the basis for viral videos. Nothing else can possibly explain South Korean Pop Star, PSY's record breaking two billion views on a trite, meaningless music video called "Gangnam Style." Pop culture renders more honor to the present cultural fad than anything of substance or long term value. Both high culture and Folk culture require an application of the fifth commandment. Myers alludes to this when he asks the question, "Could it be that one of the causes of the decline of attention to manners, those habits of behavior that allow us to demonstrate respect and honor to those to whom it is due (a Christian duty), is the triumph of popular culture's ways?"[8]

High culture, therefore, is a more highly refined form of Folk culture. An art form is honed when each successive generation stands on the shoulders of the previous generations in the developing of that art form. The deconstruction of an art form occurs as the current generation revolts against previous generations. When Andy Warhol's "Campbell's Soup Cans" paintings sold at auction for over $10 million it marked the end of high culture in America. One biographer offers this interpretation of Warhol's art form: "A group of painters have come to the common conclusion that the most banal and even vulgar trappings of modern civilization can, when transposed to canvas, become Art."[9]

However, we must take care not to designate every element of popular music in the Pop music category. There are hybrid blends everywhere. Again, Country music offers the best examples of this combination. As the star Kenny Chesney put it, "Only in Country music, you can get laid and get saved in the same three-minute song."[10] The Hank Williams dynasty (Sr., Jr. and III), illustrates the blending of popular and Folk forms. Elements of both Pop art and Folk art are present in Hank Williams Jr.'s "Whiskey Bent and Hell Bound" and "Family

Tradition." Hank III is tatted up, and the retailer Walmart routinely censors his albums for profanity, but he still records an entire album of his grandfather's songs with his father's and grandfather's voices dubbed in. Though these roots die hard, generation by generation, the destructive element of Pop culture creeps in and overwhelms the Hank family legacy.

It is hardly an exaggeration to say that most Country music singers have issued at least one entire album featuring the "old hymns of the faith," to include Johnny Cash, Charlie Pride, Jim Reeves, Moe Bandy, Randy Travis, Loretta Lynn, Alan Jackson, etc. The practice is disappearing now since the death of Johnny Cash and the first generation popular Country singers. While American Folk music morphed into the popular form, Country stars like Cash still felt an obligation to pay homage to a heritage.

When Sam Cooke debuted on the recording scene in 1951, his gospel-spiritual roots came on strong with "Hem of His Garment," "Jesus Gave Me Water," and "Peace in the Valley." His Folk themes remained for another ten years with songs like "God Bless the Child," "Danny Boy" (1958), and "Chain Gang" (1961). By 1963, his repertoire had changed dramatically as he hit the bars on "Another Saturday Night" looking for loose women where he was "Twistin' the Night Away." Artists are known best by their trajectories. Cooke was killed during an evening of drunken debauchery in 1964.

Destruction came just as quick in the Billy Ray Cyrus dynasty (another Country music star), whose daughter crossed over from Country music immediately to the Pop scene. Baptized in a Southern Baptist Church in 2005, she is better known for her drugs and fornication, as well as riding a wrecking ball more or less in the nude. Cyrus self-consciously represents the self-destructing inclinations of popular culture better than anyone else.

WHERE TO FROM HERE?

What we have today are the remnants of a civilization in which the Pop culture mentors the teens, the teens mentor their peers, and the culture is only mildly influenced by parents or pastors. The shepherds of the culture are the Pop icons, and youth pastors run hard to keep up with the cultural standards set by the icons. Is it any surprise that 70% of young men are not matured by 30 years of age (up from 30% in 1970), per Newsweek magazine, or that 80% of Christian children who are not discipled by their parents "leave the faith" after leaving home?

Where honor for parents has virtually disappeared from the consciousness of a post-Christian civilization, it is difficult to say how we will reconstruct society. Even pagan cultures maintained a rudimentary honor for parents and elders in the tribe, and this allowed for the development of culture. But the chaos that surrounds Western society is the direct result of unrelenting revolution, generation after generation.

Should a pastor or parent be concerned about the cultural decline of manners, dress, music, and other cultural forms, he does little good confronting the form directly. If the parent-child relationship is broken, if there is no honor for parents and no love for children, there is no hope for salvaging certain cultural expressions. Instead of addressing the individual manifestations of cultural decay, the pastor would do well to preach on the fifth commandment for five years, calling parents to honor grandparents, and children to honor their parents.

If pastors are called to teach men to observe each one of Christ's commandments (Matt. 28:18-20), certainly they should know something about the prevalent cultural sins. Those missionaries ministering to 19th-century South Sea islanders taught cannibals not to kill and eat each other. Those of us living in 21st-century America would do well to dust off the old commandment found in Ephesians 6:1-2. If we come upon a society like ours that has institutionalized the dishonor of parents, this must be our starting point. If parents begin the process of repentance themselves and teach their children to honor their fathers and mothers, this will be the beginning of functional churches, communities, and cultures by the next generation or two.

WHAT HAPPENS IN REAL LIFE

A personal anecdote may help to clarify what happens in the development of culture (or lack thereof). I was raised in a particularly well-regulated Christian home in the 1960s and 1970s, where my parents took special interest in limiting our access to popular culture. My father gave us three cassette tapes filled with music selections (mostly Folk), and we wore out the cassettes in my teenage years. After matriculating from homeschool into college in 1981, I purchased several albums that my parents would not have approved. I rather enjoyed them, as most other college youth were immersed in the same music. In 1990 my wife and I were married, and God blessed us with five children. As young parents, we were concerned that our children listen to "good music" and watch "decent movies." We were less concerned about ourselves than we were with our children. As my children reached their teenage years, I thought twice before introducing them to the kind of music that my wife and I had adopted in our young adult years.

Occasionally we would rent a movie that we had enjoyed in the 1980s, only to realize that the movie contained some "new" scenes that were inappropriate for our children. "I can't believe we watched that stuff back in the 80s," we would say. Several years ago, we began to "unplug" the earbuds and listen to music as a family. I found that my tastes would perceptibly change as I listened to music in the presence of my children. The accountability informed by our covenant relationship made a difference as to what I perceived to be a nurturing cultural experience, and that which I perceived not to be.

Now forty years later, it seems that I have come full circle, having returned to much of what my father and mother recommended to me in the 1960s, with a few slight modifications and "improvements." I can see how my youthful waywardness ignored the wisdom of my parents in the area of cultural expression.

INCARNATING COMMANDMENTS

Some Christians will give lip service to the fifth commandment without bothering to actually apply it in meaningful ways to their lives. They think nothing of cultural rebellion, teen rebellion, and the popularly accepted social revolutions. Parents will forfeit any interest in training or restraining their children. "I rebelled against my parents. I guess my kids will do the same thing that I did," they argue. They hardly consider what repentance might look like in regards to the fifth commandment. Their children assume that the cultural norm is acceptable, merely on the basis that "All my friends are doing it," oblivious to the direction the zeitgeist is blowing. Occasionally, Christian parents will wake up when they realize their children have become serial fornicators, homosexuals, or drug addicts. Notably, the first signals of a child's apostasy usually come with violations of the fifth commandment, in which the child refuses to submit to his or her parents' cultural standards.

In some cases, there may be little opportunity to obey the commandment, because there are no relationships left: there are no parents or other covenantal connections. Modern society has worked hard to isolate individuals in separate, hermetically-sealed containers by way of media, educational systems and economic systems. During the teenage years, family disintegration becomes the norm, and the goal of the modern family is to arrange emancipation from the home for every 18 year old daughter and son. The single years enable ample time for cultural revolution as well. Modern youth live in college dorms, Guytown or Sex-in-the-City Singleville through their twenties and thirties. Occasionally, they may return to their parents' home for Thanksgiving or Christmas, but very little cross-generational culture is transferred in aggregate.

True repentance requires some application of the fifth commandment in real life. Children must respect their parents such that they would look to their parents for wisdom in music choices, clothing, language, work habits, and entertainment options. They must seek wisdom from wise counselors in their lives, or they will play the part of the scoffer and the fool repeatedly referenced in the Book of Proverbs. At the heart of it, the Christian must act in faith in Christ. That Christian teen must come to love God and love his parents, and then follow through with obedience to the fifth commandment. Of course, faith is basic and essential. Works without true faith create hypocrisy, legalism, externalism, and apostasy.

THE ALL-ABOUT-ME POD

John C. Koss is an important man in the heartrending saga that brought about the isolation of modern man. Koss developed the first stereo headphones in 1958. For the preceding six millennia, the people of the earth had entertained themselves in communities. With his invention, a highly individualized form of entertainment entered the world. Now, individuals could immerse themselves in the cultural experience of personal amusement with ever increasing withdrawal from the community of family and friends. A few years ago, my son gave me an iPod. My wife and I went on a trip shortly afterwards, and I began listening to music using this new technology—without my wife participating. I realized that she was not enjoying the same cultural experience that I was. This "all-about-me-Pod" would never do, so then I purchased a two input splitter jack so that my wife and I could listen to the same thing together, which of course made it a "we-Pod."

Traditional dances in most cultures were organized as community circle dances, square dances, etc. By the early 1900s, couples were pairing off, and eventually, individuals were left dancing with themselves on the dance floor. Long-term marriages gave way to divorce. Temporary shack-ups gave way to increasingly transient hook-ups. Parents and children who used to listen to the radio or watch television together in the 1950s, were now listening to their own music on their individual iPods, and watching their own individualized entertainment fare on their iPads and in-bedroom television sets.

Jean Paul Sartre's existentialism created a new persona for the modern man. This person is the brave lone warrior who has abandoned meaningful relationship with family and community. He is the Jack Bauer of television series 24. He is James Bond, John McClane, and Dirty Harry. He is Bob Dylan's "Rolling Stone." He is a stranger in the night exchanging glances with some other stranger. He is a lone divorcee cop who finds his only identity in the police force and he saves the world again and again in each new television episode. In these images, the modern finds his ideal. This is what he aspires to be as he escapes into a pretend world of music, movies, and internet, creating new experiences, new culture, and new relationships with each pretend persona. He gradually loses his personality at the same time the others lose theirs.

When man forsakes relationship with God in the vertical, it is not long before he kills relationship with his brother in the horizontal. Three chapters into the Book of Genesis, Adam broke relationship with God; in the very next chapter, Cain killed his brother. After that, the Lord God consigned Cain to the wilderness, where he built the first city of anonymity and wandered like a vagabond somewhere "east of Eden." Thus, Jean-Paul Sartre's authentic existentialist lives alone, "entirely alone." He "never speaks to anyone, never. . ."[11] Modern man has captured this ideal better than anyone, except perhaps Cain, the prototype vagabond. "Man became a stranger to himself, to his fellowman, and a vagabond on the earth, exiled from his true home, the paradise of God."[12]

How many science fiction novels must a man read before he lives in a reality far separate from his own family? How many hours must he plug himself into the internet or the television set before he loses contact with real people? One rarely sees boys working in the fields with their fathers or even playing ball in the sandlots anymore. Teenage girls sit in restaurants texting each other from across the same table. Their relationships are painfully shallow; dry as parched earth.

The most popular motion picture of all time, *Avatar*, released in 2009, tells the story of a man who abandons his true personality to take on the pseudo-personality of his "avatar." The movie grossed almost $3 billion in worldwide box office receipts. On the internet, an "avatar" is a small icon representing a person, and is usually used for playing a virtual game online. How many of the personalities that interact on the internet are false personas? Billions of youth create online personalities for themselves, and eventually they identify more with their pseudo-personalities than they do with their real personalities. Even the stars on the movie screen present false personalities. This phenomenon demonstrates the utterly desperate condition of modern man.

Why all this isolation, as man cuts himself off from all real people? Like Adam and Eve, modern man hides from God in the garden. Sartre described this worldview better than anybody else, as he declared, "Hell is other people," in that other people are inescapably revelatory of the image of God. Modern man attempts to escape his own reality, because his own reality is another painful reminder of the image of God, who he must avoid at all costs.

> "And Cain said unto the Lord, 'My punishment is greater than I can bear. Behold, thou hast driven me out this day from the face of the earth; and from thy face shall I be hid; and I shall be a fugitive and a vagabond in the earth.'" (Gen. 4:13-14)

8: Wise Discernment for Music in Home and Church

As it turns out, the Bible does not condemn Pop music or Rock n' Roll. Nevertheless, the moral mandates of Scripture are still important and relevant to music, and all Christians will "keep the commandments of God" until the end (Rev. 14:12). The big picture principles of Scripture apply to music as much as to everything else in life. For example, "Honor thy father and mother" applies to the music choices in the home. "Thou shalt not commit adultery" applies as much to the false prophets of popular music as it does to anybody else. The fear of God is as much the beginning of knowledge and wisdom in the university classroom as it is in the composer's study. In all things, whether eating, drinking or singing, we are to do all to the glory of God (1 Cor. 10:31).

WHAT THE BIBLE SAYS SPECIFICALLY ABOUT MUSIC

Sincere, careful Christians want to be cautious not to give way to simplistic arguments, or guilt-by-association logical fallacies in their treatment of cultural expressions. There are many versions of autonomy. When Christian leaders forbid alcohol, dancing, movies, as *malum in se* (sinful in themselves), it is not long before man's laws displace God's laws, and we are left with one more form of autonomous rebellion against God. This antinomian fundamentalism has done immeasurable damage to the church. Hence, we must think carefully and biblically when it comes to culture. Refusing to apply God's laws at all is another form of autonomy and this too is unacceptable for Christians. What then does the Bible say about music? Since there are only a handful of verses in Scripture that provide specific instruction concerning music and method, we will focus on these. It does not appear that music carries a central role in the New Testament church, as it does in most of the evangelical church today. Yet, it is sufficiently important to be mentioned in Scripture, and if God has something to say about it, we had better listen.

Generally, according to Scripture music and dancing are employed for times of joyful celebration in community (1 Sam. 18:6, Eccl. 12:4, Luke 15:25). The primary use for music in the Old Testament is worship (1 Chron. 15:16, 2 Chron. 5:13, 7:6). The New Testament provides three verses that address the use of music, as follows:

> "*Speaking to yourselves in Psalms and hymns and spiritual songs, singing and making melody in your heart to the Lord.*" (Eph. 5:19)

> "*Let the Word of Christ dwell in you richly in all wisdom; teaching and admonishing one another in Psalms and hymns and spiritual songs, singing with grace in your hearts to the Lord.*" (Col. 3:16)

> "*What is it then? I will pray with the spirit, and I will pray with the understanding also; I will sing with the spirit, and I will sing with the understanding also, else...the other is not edified.*" (1 Cor. 14:15)

Based on this corpus of biblical content on music, the following lessons are drawn:

1. Music is a community event. Paul's concern is that *others* are edified, instructed, and admonished in music. Also in Deuteronomy chapters 12 and 16, God commands celebration and entertainment for his people. However, in both cases the rejoicing must occur "before the Lord" and in community with sons, daughters, widows, and Levites. We sing "to the Lord' and to others. The expectation is that nobody holes up in a corner by himself with his iPod and his beer, and gets drunk. Thus, entertainment must take place before the face of God (with a spirit of rejoicing and thanksgiving), and in the presence of others. This is much different than Sartre's lone existentialist who crawls inside of himself to die.

Singing as demonstrated in the Old Testament is done within the context of public worship. Of course, this does not preclude believers singing to themselves throughout the day, but the emphasis is other-oriented.

2. Music is meant to exhort. Interestingly, Paul does not regard music as a means to make us feel good or to give us an emotional boost, although this may have been the use of it with Saul when he was afflicted by evil spirits (1 Sam. 16:23). Instead, for the Apostles, music must be a means by which we admonish each other, internalize the Word of God, and then obey it. Although it might come across as odd to the modern romanticized ear, Paul might recommend singing, "Thou shalt not commit adultery," with the expectation that we follow through on these words and live pure lives. The song may not provide us with a warm and fuzzy feeling and it may not offer much in entertainment value, but it may help to affirm one of the commandments.

3. The primary content recommended in the biblical admonition is "the Word of Christ" (Col. 3:16). This does not eliminate all content surrounding Christ, but somehow Christ must remain the focal point.

4. Psalm singing is commanded. There is no debate as to whether Psalms are included in the list delineated in Colossians 3:16 and Ephesians 5:19. While church history supports a predominant psalmody stance, other songs are clearly acceptable in Scripture and early church historical record.

5. Music calls for mind and spirit. "I will sing with the understanding also." Since the 19th century, specifically after Richard Wagner's revolutionary work, artistic expression increasingly sought to invoke a purely emotional response. Music became a conduit for unrestrained emotional release. Set a recording of a 17th century choral piece next to the screaming, pretentious, frenzied, unbridled passion of a popular Rock song and you will hear the contrast immediately. The 17th century piece sounds restrained and boring to the ear of the modern teen. While the historic Christian church saw music merely as a vessel to contain content and exhortation, humanist man

became focused on the vessel itself. It really didn't matter whether the vessel contained words that commended fornication or Christ. The words were supplementary or incidental. The same vessel was used for either message. What mattered was the vessel itself, not what the vessel contained. What was important was how the music made us feel or how it affirmed our feelings.

In one of the few passages available on a method for prayer, Jesus forbids prayer and worship that contains vain repetition "as the heathen do" (Matt. 6:7). Heathen worship typically consists of relentless repetition in mantras, words, phrases, or rhythms. The Christian must resist this form of worship and music. Intensive repetition leads to hypnosis, a disconnection of the mind or understanding from the content—and this 1 Corinthians 12 strictly forbids. If the Bible offers any wisdom and any pattern at all for worship music, we should take note that God's revelation never repeats a word successively more than three times. "Holy, holy, holy." A chorus between verses is used once or twice in 150 Psalms.

Somehow, the majestic words of the historic hymns were lost to the 21st century mind. The Gen X Christian youth hoped that if he could put them to new, exciting, frenzied tunes, he might somehow recapture the meaning contained in the words. But alas, the experiment hasn't proven as successful as he had hoped. The zeitgeist eschews meaning.

This is the corpus of biblical teaching on music and singing. That being the case, the contemporary musician in the church should honestly assess his choices. Does the music teach and exhort, as its primary function? Have the "vain repetitions" characteristic of heathen music crept into Christian worship? While biblical authors do not use "highly technical" language in their evaluation of good music, an honest assessment of Christian music, based on these simple matters is in order. Do people actively engage their minds with the truths contained in the words of the music? Or do they turn off and just sway to the music, emoting to the feel of the rhythm, melody, and words?

WORSHIP MUSIC

As already pointed out, Christian music is meant to instruct and admonish, first and foremost. The music provides a context in which the Word of Christ may dwell in us richly. We assume that Paul intends for us to sing to each other every day, throughout the day. Although recorded music may be legitimate, Paul still wants real people singing to and with other real people, brothers and sisters in Christ. Given that 1 Corinthians 14 addresses the public worship of the church, the Apostle clearly expects singing to occur in the worship service (vs. 15).

When it comes to worship music, the fear of God is essential. That may be expressed in a catacomb or in a cathedral; and the music form will differ depending on context. There is a fear in worship that expresses itself in more grandiose praise, and there is that fear that expresses itself in quiet, humble, and somber tones. Naturally, the musical approach will give expression to the situation. Some conditions call for pipe organs, for example, and others for a cappella or simple guitar accompaniment. True worshipers will reject all pride, showmanship, insincerity, empty emotions, and man-pleasing entertainment (as opposed to God-pleasing worship). Does contemporary Christian music produce God-acceptable worship? What about the Mormon Tabernacle choir singing The Messiah? How does the liberal mainline church with its pipe organ compare with the evangelical church with a worship band in the rented warehouse down the street? Ultimately, God will judge. Considering the present day apostasy, seeing that regular church attendance for millennials has fallen to 18%,[1] how can we be sure that the new evangelical worship style will salvage the faith? At this point, every church left in the Western world ought to be on its knees pleading for God's mercy upon the remnant and seeking His wisdom.

The recent worship song "I Could Sing of Your Love Forever" repeats the title line fifteen to twenty times consecutively.[2] This may be a record in the history of "sacred" music. In one verse, the songwriter opens up his own heart to "let the healer set me free." That is unbiblical language, prima facie. Where in the Gospel is Jesus begging people to open up their hearts, so he can set them free and heal their blindness? Actually, according to the biblical testimony, God hardens hearts and blinds the eyes and sets the captives free. Place a song like this next to "A Mighty Fortress Is Our God", and ask yourself if we are truly seeing improvements in such things as biblical content, the avoidance of vain repetition, admonition and teaching, sharpening the acuity of understanding, and setting forth of biblical truth? Are we improving or degrading in these key areas ordained by God for our music? Given the fractured mind of the electronic generation, not many millennials are capable of following lyrical statements containing more than twenty words, or four to five   distinct theological concepts in a single verse. If anything, the maturity of mind and understanding for the average professing Christian is far lower today than it was one hundred years ago.

A survey of the most popular "worship" songs according to the up-to-date list maintained by CCLI (Christian Copyright Licensing International) reveals big differences between the current worship music genre and the hymns of the last millennium of the church. A statistical analysis of the traditional hymns and Psalms of the church as compared to the latest Redman/Tomlin/etc. fare revealed marked differences.

The individual word repetition ratio (as determined by word count as a fraction of word frequency count) for contemporary songs was 6.02 compared to 2.30 for the hymns and Psalms. That is, each word was repeated over 6 times on average in the modern selections, a frequency much higher than that used in the old hymns and Psalms. This repetition marks the most significant difference for modern worship music.

Also, the modern choruses used the words "I," "me," "my," "we," and "us," 201 times, with only 91 references to "You," "Yours" and "His." The old hymns and Psalms of David in the sample included only 32 uses of "me", my," "I," and "we," with 56 references to "You," "He," and "His." Based on these straightforward statistics, the me-centricity of the new worship songs are 3.28 times higher than what we find in music from the historic Christian church. Or, put another way, the old hymns speak of self half as often as they speak about God, while the modern choruses speak of self twice as often as they speak about God. This represents a radical departure from a God-centered worldview, and sincere Christians should take note. The average sentence length (or phrase following a subject line) for the traditional hymns and Psalms was 15.95 words, compared to 6.8 for the newer musical selections. Is the modern Christian mind capable of absorbing the words and concepts contained in the Psalms, and how well might this truth be retained through life? We wonder.

Do these cultural developments in our generation represent good trajectories for the Western faith, or do they illustrate fragmentation and dissolution of faith? While there may be a few healthy strands of church culture here and there, the West stays on a trajectory towards more man-centered humanism and general apostasy.

The reader may note that this critique of the modern church music phenomenon does not appeal to arguments that point out "Satanic" African roots, the promotion of "lustful sensuality," etc. Rather, all of us must submit to biblical principles in relation to music, worship, and church sociology. How do the cultural revolutions help to integrate the generations, such that older women are able to mentor younger women, and older men mentor the younger men in the church? (Tit. 2:1-8). Are we submitting to biblical patterns in the area of vain repetition? How does the modern worshiper engage the whole mind in the worship service? Does biblical truth frame our worship, or is it something else?

An honest and conscientious application of biblical principle to family and church culture is of essence. If the commandments of God are ignored, then we will fall into sins of omission and commission even if hardly anybody recognizes it. The decline of Christian culture therefore, in family and church, must have something to do with the fact that too many Christians have ignored the laws of God for a long time. Could it be that a theological antipathy to the law of God is at the root of cultural decline? God's Word does not separate loving God and keeping His commandments (John 15:10, 1 John 5:3, 2 John 6), and it certainly does not separate faith and works (Jas. 2:26).

9: Entertainment and Metaphor

Human beings experience life in three different realities or three different planes: the spiritual, the physical, and the metaphor. Effectively, these make up the existential metaphysic, reality as perceived by the individual. More than ever, 21st century man confuses the physical plane and the metaphor (the imaginary world). This confusion is nicely illustrated in the 2011 Christopher Nolan film, *Inception*. As the viewers watch the movie, they lose track of what is happening in the dream state and what is happening in reality while they themselves are transported into the non-reality of the film metaphor. Lines between the metaphor and physical reality are ever more blurred in the mind of the post-modern.

Avatar (2009) broke the all-time box office record by introducing a new twist in fantasy film, expertly enhanced with visual effects. Most of the movie took place in a dream state, nicely accomodating the market needs of a post-modern, escapist society. As the audience is taken into the metaphor to watch an actor play the part of a fantasy character, the lead is placed into a dream state in which he plays the part of another fantasy character. Although all are not affected equally by these forces, films like this teach post-modern entertainment junkies to prefer the dream state over reality.

The Christian understands reality via two symbiotic aspects: by physical sensation in the physical world, and by spiritual interpretation that assumes the biblical supernatural metaphysic. We as Christians do not understand essential evil as "a serial killer," for example. Rather, we define evil in spiritual terms, by words like "sin," "the transgression of the law of God," "sinful nature," and "demonic powers." In the words of the Apostle, "we wrestle not against flesh and blood, but against principalities, against powers, against the rulers of the darkness of this world, against spiritual wickedness in high places" (Eph. 6:12). We define all of God's acts in history as acts of justice or judgment. Natural events then, have a supernatural component to them. Therefore we do not see the world merely in terms of physical actions and reactions. We see that there is something of significance going on, something happening behind the scenes, something that is intertwined into the real events playing out before us.

The remainder of this chapter will examine the plane of metaphor. All artistic expression is metaphor in that it never creates *ex nihilo* (out of nothing), but merely discovers what God has already created. The artist must think God's thoughts after Him if he will do any true art.

> *"It is the glory of God to conceal a thing: but the honor of kings to search out a matter. The heaven for height, and the earth for depth and the heart of the king is unsearchable."* (Prov. 25:2-3)

Every scientist, writer, and artist fills an honorable role insomuch as they search out those matters concealed in God's creation, to include the complexities of human nature. Therefore, good art will reflect God's thoughts and God's reality. When art fails to accomplish this task, it becomes destructive rather than creative. Twentieth century Christian scholar, R.J. Rushdoony describes man's quest for knowledge:

> "God having made all things, nothing exists in and of itself. Thus, to attempt an abstraction is to attempt the impossible. Nothing has any residue of being or meaning which can be abstracted from God and His created purpose. Every atom of every particular thing is a creation of God, and it is only truly knowable in terms of Him. To attempt the interpretation of anything without God is impossible. The unbeliever, seeking knowledge, if he is faithful to his premises, can know nothing, because he has denied any purpose, order, or meaning in the universe by denying God...Because man is

created in the image of God, it is suicidal for man to try to escape from the knowledge of God. Man is drawn to knowledge as a plant to the sun; if the plant turns from the sun, it is wilting and will die. Thus, an aspect of man's revolt against maturity and against life is his revolt against knowledge. Whereas man may seek knowledge as a substitute for God and as a means of becoming God, he soon turns from knowledge itself because it is inescapably revelational of God."[1]

Herein lies the tension that tears at the heart of unbelieving artists. Literary men such as Ernest Hemingway, Percy Shelley, and Hunter S. Thompson set out on a safari through the jungle of the world in search of true knowledge. As they approach a clearing revealing the sun of truth, they instinctively turn away from it. They proceed to blaze another trail through the jungle until they find another clearing, but again the truth they discover is revelational of God. Eventually, they either lose themselves in the jungle or commit suicide.

ENTERTAINMENT AND AMUSEMENT

If art is metaphor, then modern entertainment and amusement increasingly turns art into diversion and escape. Modern life demands diversion on a continual basis. Over four hundred years ago, the French philosopher Michel de Montaigne called for constant diversion to save natural man from the psychosis of isolation. "Variety always solaces, dissolves, and scatters. By changing place, occupation, company, I escape into the crowd of other thoughts and diversions where it loses my trace, and leaves me safe."[2] Here is a good definition for the internet in the life of the average 40 year old, and 14 year old, and 4 year old. One hundred years ago, human beings could not possibly change their "place, occupation, and company" every two seconds—now they can.

For many years, the best escape from reality was drunkenness or drug addictions. However, with the electronics revolution of the 20th century, all that changed. A thousand exit ramps off the highway of reality are now available to the masses. Until the 19th century, people were forced to connect in real communities and families. They enjoyed some aesthetics in the form of art, theater, and live concerts. Following the 18th century, there came a flood of novels, science fiction, sports, motion pictures, television, and the internet. Much of this was intended to provide escape routes into the metaphor.

The postmodern man experiences *Groundhog Day* every day, like Bill Murray in the film by the same name; it is a repetitive, pointless existence because it isn't real. Bill Murray's character wakes up each day on the same day as yesterday, and he relives that day in different ways. The postmodernist lives in the meta-narrative. He laughs at himself laughing. He laughs at himself crying. Eventually he will un-friend his best friend on Facebook without thinking about it twice, because everything is valueless at the end of the day.

A recent poll conducted by The Barna Group found that only 0.5% of American young people (ages 18-25) believe in absolutes, as compared to 14% in the previous generation.[3] In the public forum today whether on the street or in the university classroom, the highest form of heresy is to state a truth or advocate a moral position with any hint of dogmatism. That is a given. The final step for the postmodernist is to deny that there is an absolute quality to reality. As truth and ethics fade, reality also fades with them.

The archetypal postmodern man walks into church and listens to a sermon in which the preacher is still connected with true and ultimate reality. It seems that the preacher can almost feel for himself the gusts of heat blowing out of the fires of hell. The voice from the pulpit is tinged with fear of God, urgency, and concern for human souls. So the postmodernist sits down and listens. He is riveted. He calls for more popcorn. This is better than the latest horror flick he watched...*Friday the 13th*, "Part 27." For this fellow, nothing is real. Hell isn't real, because nothing is real. The preacher isn't real. God isn't real. And he himself isn't real. He is entirely submerged in the metaphor.

Those who are still in contact with reality will recognize *this scenario* to be the highest form of horror. In this sad account of the postmodern man, the most real experience he will ever encounter will happen when he awakens at the judgment seat of Christ and hears the words, "Depart from me, you cursed, you workers of iniquity!" According to Deuteronomy 7:10, God will judge that man "to the face," and he will receive his final sentence in full awareness and sense of its force. There will be no drugs to cushion the experience or to numb its effects. Thus, I hope my reader can see the frightening condition of the man who is past feeling towards God, judgment, and his own existence (Eph. 4:19).

This postmodern reminds us of the man who went on a honeymoon, but when he returned, he only spoke of the cruise, the food, and the entertainment. We asked him about his wife, and he couldn't seem to remember that she was there. What sort of a wretch would marry a woman and forget her presence on the honeymoon? This is a man who has lost touch with reality. Similarly, natural man in the fallen state walks out into God's world and forgets about God. When the reality of God fades in man's consciousness, the reality of everything else fades with it.

However, postmodern man retains something of a love-hate relationship with reality. He often escapes it, but from time to time, he desires to reach out to touch something real. He reacts to what Sartre would refer to as the "horror of nonexistence." So he seeks increasingly intensive thrills at amusement parks as the rides yank him around at 3, 4, or 5 G's. He leaps out of airplanes, and bungee jumps off of bridges.

All of this post-modernist relativism is foolishness, of course. This man is still hiding behind the trees in the garden of Eden. If he pretends that he does not exist, maybe God will forget about him too, or so he thinks. I knew a family that had forbidden their dog to enter the carpeted living room. While everybody watched, the dog would place his paws over his eyes and wiggle himself into forbidden territory. In the end, all of his mental gymnastics were only pathetic attempts to avoid the most obvious realities. The postmodernist, like the dog covering his eyes as he disobeys his master, is still suppressing the truth in unrighteousness (Rom. 1:18).

THE CHRISTIAN AND THE ZEITGEIST

If you happen to frequent a department store during Black Friday sales, you may note that the mob typically congregates in the electronics department. They show much less interest in clothing, house wares, and jewelry. It seems that men and women are far more interested in the electronic universe than they are in kitchen supplies, hardware, knitting, toys, and socks. In the 1950s, young men would rise at 6:00AM, put on their suits and ties, and go off to college to make their fortune in the world. Now, young men play games and disengage. In September of 2013, the world witnessed the largest, single, entertainment rollout in the world when Grand Theft Auto V released.[4] This video game raked in $1 billion in just three days. In constant dollars, the worldwide computer game industry has grown from $2 billion in 1982 to an estimated $93 billion in 2014 and should exceed $120 billion in three years.[5] These numbers far exceed the size of the music industry ($40 billion), the movie industry ($27 billion), and the book industry ($63 billion).

Hour for hour, computer games consume more time for Americans, Japanese, and Koreans than movies and perhaps even music. A recent study found that Americans now spend 4 hours and 40 minutes a day online, and 4 hours and 31 minutes a day watching television. Internet access time has increased 28% in just three years.[6] At least 60% of their waking hours are consumed by media. If they work or study for the other 7-8 hours in the day, there is no time left to invest in their relationships with others. Media is depersonalizing society. Even if a family watches television together (which doesn't happen very often), they are still individually absorbed in another world, and less and less communicating with one another.

How does the Christian interact with culture when the spirit of the age is fully given over to the escape from reality and relationships? If most of the food sold at the butcher is food offered to idols, what does the Christian do with this food? How does the Christian operate within this zeitgeist? If the audiovisual medium is almost completely dedicated to escape, what can the Christian do with this medium? "All things are lawful, but not all things are expedient," that is all things are not wise and profitable. For example, I personally wouldn't have a problem with a Christian business selling hemp (or marijuana) for rope or for hemp cloth diapers (which, I understand, retain higher than average absorbent qualities). But setting up a hemp shop in the inner city amid rows of rundown apartment buildings may not be the best strategy for the believer. No doubt business would be brisk, but I doubt that the clientele would be much interested in diapers and rope. Does the Christian want to aid the escape from reality, whether by drugs or by media? For this reason, Christians are sometimes hesitant to own liquor stores; they fear that the majority of the clientele would overindulge.

Therefore, Christian leaders in media will always favor preaching, documentaries, and real conversations between real people. Dramatic film will highlight historical events because they are strongly connected with true reality, God's reality, or God's story played out in human history. If the heathen are affirming some sort of non-reality in their temples of film, then it is for us to describe more of God's reality in God's reality. This is why movies like *The Hiding Place*, *Return to the Hiding Place*, and *Hotel Rwanda* were jarring and effective at communicating a message. Whereas the movie *Avatar* tells no real story, has no bona fide tyrant, and offers no efficacious redemption, the Christian-produced *Return to the Hiding Place* provides all that. Moreover, these stories were based on true historical events. This itself keeps the audience connected with God's reality at least in some form.

SPORTS IS METAPHOR

Historically, sports have provided a metaphor for warfare. Whether it was the Scottish caber toss, the Aztec Ullamaliztli ball game, or the Roman competitions, the connection to warfare in the origins is undeniable. Nations and empires are primarily interested in defending themselves and winning their battles. Collegiate and professional sports provide a venue in which to cultivate the competitive spirit and train the physical prowess necessary for battle. It is also true that sporting activities provide needed exercise for those who live otherwise sedentary lives.

Nonetheless, the purpose of modern sports has mainly become

entertainment. Spectator sports supply little benefit for the fat man in the La-Z-Boy recliner sipping on his six-pack while he roots for his team. Vast numbers of men in our day are thoroughly absorbed in the metaphor of sports, and take little interest in the real wars. Sadly, many fathers ignore the spiritual powers that are constantly undermining liberty, destroying morality, and eroding family life in the 21st century. Using hyperbole to illustrate the point, suppose there was a fellow watching his game while his daughter is attacked either physically or spiritually by a gang of thugs on the street. At this point in his life, what matters most to the man is that his team wins. If his son is playing a video game in the basement, he cares little about the plight of his sister, because he is about to make it to the 17th level in his video game. The modern father loses perspective. His daughter joins the army to defend the nation while he watches the Cowboys play the Raiders. He is utterly lost in the metaphor, and has no taste for the real spiritual battles of life.

When our family watches a handful of men defending their loved ones against ten thousand evil beasts on the movie screen, my blood temperature rises a bit. This battle scene is reminiscent of the real battles we engage every day against the principalities and powers that seek to dominate in our own hearts and families, and in many of the governments in the western world. There is a use for stories and metaphor, but if they disconnect us from the reality of life, then we are sleeping on the enchanted ground in the midst of a most critical war. The important question we must ask ourselves about each entertaining event in which we participate is: Does this entertainment connect us with the proper metaphysic or disconnect us from it? As we participate, are we more in touch with true reality, or less so?

When Christian men and their families are more impressed by a sports hero who throws a ball a few yards than they are with a Christian martyr in Iran, we wonder if perhaps somebody is losing touch with reality. What would the church fathers think of Christians who are more impressed by the gladiator games than by the martyrs dying in the same arena?

LEGITIMATE METAPHOR

The Bible is filled with metaphor. The Red Sea experience is a phenomenal story of deliverance, but it must remind us of Christ's redemption or we have missed the major point. Jesus spoke in parables, which always pointed to an important spiritual truth. Several literary works outside of the Bible also have parable-like stories: *The Pilgrim's Progress*, which is metaphoric of the Christian life, and *Beowulf*, strongly metaphoric of spiritual battle with the devil (and filled with biblical language).

In his short article "On Fairy Stories," J.R.R. Tolkien explains that the fantasy genre is a natural derivative of our created state in the image of God: "Fantasy remains a human right: we make in our measure and in our derivative mode, because we are made: and not only made, but made in the image and likeness of a Maker." He speaks of a healthy "recovery" and "escape" in the story, in which we connect with true reality, and we begin "seeing things as we are (or were) meant to see them."[7]

He refers to the Christian story of the Gospels as the "supreme" story, then he acknowledges the absolute sovereignty of God over all: "It is true. Art has been verified. God is the Lord, of angels, and of men—and of elves."[8] This makes for a critical statement in regards to Tolkein's fictional works, in that he places God squarely in the metaphysic. He understands that man in a sinful estate doesn't quite get the story straight. Yet, in a Christian age, the fallenness of man and the redemption of man both play a part in the story.

Tolkien continues, "Legend and History have met and fused. But in God's kingdom the presence of the greatest does not depress the small. Redeemed Man is still man. Story, fantasy, still go on, and should go on. The Evangelium has not abrogated legends; it has hallowed them, especially the 'happy ending.' The Christian has still to work, with mind as well as body, to suffer, hope, and die; but he may now perceive that all his bents and faculties have a purpose, which can be redeemed. So great is the bounty with which he has been treated that he may now, perhaps, fairly dare to guess that in Fantasy he may actually assist in the effoliation and multiple enrichment of creation. All tales may come true; and yet, at the last, redeemed, they may be as like and as unlike the forms that we give them as Man, finally redeemed, will be like and unlike the fallen that we know."[9]

While stories may themselves play a part in the redemption of all creation, can we say that the "happy ending" is enough to make for a good story? I would still argue that metaphor can be done badly if it breaks God's laws with impunity and without remorse.

WHERE METAPHOR ERRS

In a later chapter, we will consider the evaluation of film and literature using biblical ethical categories in more detail. For now, we will submit metaphor itself and the fantasy genre to the ethical constraints of God's laws. To operate or to pretend to operate entirely outside of the dominion of the supreme God and His laws is to play the devil's game. This constituted Satan's original temptation: "Ye shall be as gods, determining good and evil for yourself." Autonomy is the attempt to create ones' own definitions of good and evil or right and wrong, and the temptation plays strong in the mind of natural man.

To this day, the Harry Potter film series maintains the worldwide record for box office sales at $7.7 billion, and the Twilight series takes second place at $3.3 billion. On July 21, 2007, the final book in the series, *Harry Potter and the Deathly Hallows*, set the world record for the highest, single day sales, with 8.3 million copies. The previous record was set by a different Harry Potter book, released two years earlier (at 6.9 million copies).[10] Those who want to follow the worldviews that capture the hearts and minds of the masses will identify this as the zeitgeist of the day. The heroes and heroines of these stories are witches or vampires. Harry Potter is a wizard, trained by a homosexual by the name of Dumbledore. All the homosexuals and witches in these stories are commended for their "kindness," "justice," "mercy," "integrity," and "love;" yet when these terms show up in these stories, they are not recognizable as the same virtues as defined by God's law. The Christian apologists who rush to defend Harry Potter, Dumbledore, and their ilk always assume the humanist categories of virtue and ethics. Those who refuse to employ biblical ethics and biblical definitions to establish the thesis and antithesis are fundamentally anti-Christian. Antinomianism in America has resulted in a high level of apostasy in the seminaries, churches, and theaters.

Christian devotees of Harry Potter want to assume that the metaphorical context excuses everything. They think that the protagonists are exempt from the constraints of biblical law as long as they are confined to their own world of metaphor. The author becomes the de facto sovereign, and she can do whatever she wants to do in her world. Thus, Harry Potter the Witch may just as well be Harry Potter the Fornicator, or Harry Potter the Rapist. If Harry Potter breathes out spells, enchantments, or whisperings (Deut. 18:10), by biblical definition he is a witch. The same applies to sexual sin. Whether or not he lives in a parallel universe, if a man is sexually involved with a woman outside of marriage, by biblical definition he is a fornicator. It matters not a whit that he plays the part of the hero in the imaginary tale. It does not matter that he is an alien. In a recent *Star Trek* blockbuster, Captain Kirk, the hero of the series, fornicates with not one, but two alien beings. By biblical definition, this is confusion, abominable, unmentionable, and even criminal activity (Lev. 20:15-16; Deut. 22:10, 27:21). The pagan producers passed it off as a social faux pas,[11] so as to soften the audience to more sexual confusion. If the cultural trajectory is set by ethical relativism and sexual confusion, must Christians participate? Many Christians have already committed themselves emotionally to the *Star Trek* series which self-professedly assumes an evolutionary construct and allows for complete ethical relativism and intra-species mating. Do some of these cultural vehicles pave the way to apostasy?

Within the fantasy genre, the use of the words "wizard" and "witch" is problematic for the same reason that we would not want to have a "rapist" or an "ax murderer" playing the part of the hero. According to the title chosen for Harry Potter, and according to the description of his role as a wizard, we must conclude that Harry Potter's wizard-ness is a sin against God. The real core problem with witchcraft is that it seeks power, particularly special and supernatural power, apart from God. In the Harry Potter story, there is no God identified as the ultimate source of spiritual and physical power. Rather, the source of power is the tail of the Phoenix Bird, and both hero and villain obtain power from the same source. "Fawkes gave two feathers, which ended up in the wands of Harry Potter and Lord Voldemort, which is said to be the reason why they locked in Priori Incantatem when the two wizards attempted to engage in a magical battle in the Little Hangleton graveyard."[12] How this differs from an African witch doctor in his attempts to conjure up power from the material universe is anybody's guess. The battles between wizards hardly mean anything if the ultimate source of power and ethics has been dispensed with. Some apologists for Harry Potter will draw distinctions between incantational and invocational magic, or mechanical and occultist magic, yet this doesn't address the fundamental questions. What is the professed source of power in the story? Are the witches muttering or whispering occultist spells? Why do Harry Potter and his witch friends ride brooms?

If the author calls it a duck, if it quacks like a duck, it really must be a duck. If the author calls the hero a rapist, and the rapist does what rapists do, then we have to conclude that the protagonist is committing capital crimes and should be dealt with accordingly. It doesn't matter if he saves somebody's life, avoids backing over little old ladies in a parking lot, and smacks down serial killers in the process of the story. He's still a rapist.

The outing of Harry Potter's mentor, Dumbledore in 2007 was well-timed.[13] Author J.K. Rowling waited until the series was complete and millions of fans were emotionally attached to the characters before she made the announcement that "Dumbledore is gay." Rowling is quoted, in a tweet published on December 16, 2014, "If Harry Potter taught us anything it's that no one should live in a closet."[14] That an author who had endorsed witchcraft would endorse another abomination (homosexuality), is no big surprise, I suppose. Her plan fit nicely into the well-orchestrated, worldwide adoption of the homosexual agenda. This announcement pressed some Christian leaders to distance themselves from the series, but others kept up an enthusiastic support for Rowling's work.[15] If a character is presented in the story as defined in a positive light by witchcraft and homosexuality, without any hint that he repents or should repent, then there must be a powerful evil force at work upon the millions of men, women, and children who are drawn into the web. If Christians are more interested in endorsing these cultural deviations than demolishing imaginations and strongholds, apostasy must be in full swing.

Modern Christians seem to want to spend more time identifying hidden, esoteric metaphors in these godless stories that are supposed to signify some Christian truth, but we do not find the church fathers doing this with the Greek myths and the Greek gods. Too many modern church leaders would rather admire the artistic work of the idol manufacturers in Ephesus, while forgetting that these idols are still idols! Is the Harry Potter tale a Christian story filled with Christian symbols and sacraments as some have suggested, or are the dogs licking up the communion wine at the table? The devil is a clever imp, and it would be well that Christians would answer questions like this truthfully.

It wasn't until the second installment of the winsome and popular, *How to Train Your Dragon*, that the producers of this film series outed Gobber as a homosexual. In the first episode, millions of Christian children were introduced to Gobber as the likable mentor for the young hero, Hiccup. Eerily familiar to the pederasty of the old Greek gymnasium, a pattern emerges in Dumbledore and Gobber, both homosexual mentors for the young boy protagonists in extremely popular films. Now in the 21st century, the cultural powers have discovered that there is more than one way to corrupt boys and girls. It used to happen in the Greek gymnasium; now it happens in popular children's books and films. They may not understand or embrace all the nuances of the stories in their younger years, however that is the age at which their alliances and affections are developed. By the time they are adults, they will find it impossible to condemn Dumbledore and Gobber for their sexual proclivities.

For the record, the use of the term "wizard" for Gandalf in J.R.R.

Tolkien's *Lord of the Rings* series is also problematic. There may be some debate over Gandalf's "magic" and the source of magical power as defined by the author. Nonetheless, the spells or whisperings of Radagast contained in several of the recent Hobbit films parallel the biblical definitions of witchcraft found in Deuteronomy 18:10. At one point in the film, the wizard actually refers to his own spell casting as a form of witchcraft! It is interesting, however, that these scenes in the movie were not originally found in Tolkien's works.

The Bible does not condemn the creation of endearing characters like hobbits, dwarves, elves, and the like. Nor does the Bible condemn the use of witches in stories, as long as the line between good and evil is clearly understood. Moreover, there is nothing wrong with putting personalities and voices to donkeys, horses, and ducks. The reader will remember that Balaam was addressed by his donkey in Numbers 22. Nonetheless, there are lines over which writers must not transgress, even in fantasy literature. If a quality or action considered sinful by the law of God is presented in a good light, then we are calling evil good, and good evil (Isa. 5:20).

The outrageously popular Twilight series of books and films feature a young woman who is drawn to vampirism. While the books are touted for their "high sexual tension," we also find a strong pull towards the pagan rite of blood consumption. The story tries to maintain a thin, ineffectual distinction between the "good" and "bad" vampires—the good guys stick to consuming animal blood. Nonetheless, according to biblical law in both Old Testament and New Testament, the pagan rite of blood consumption is prohibited (Lev. 17:10-12, Deut. 12:23-25, Acts 15:20).

As the Twilight story progresses, the draw towards vampirism is so strong that the heroine eventually concedes, to the delight of millions of teen girl pagan wanna-be's. Such metaphors provide a sharp antithetical contrast with the biblical story of redemption; for we receive eternal life by the voluntary offering of Christ's blood, not by the pseudo-salvation story of paganism and the consumption of animal or human blood on the part of the walking dead (who cannot tolerate walking in the light).

"Beware lest any man spoil you through philosophy and vain deceit, after the tradition of men, after the rudiments of the world, and not after Christ." (Col. 2:8)

The collapse of the Christian faith in the present generation is far more a matter of culture than politics. Hollywood and Nashville producers are a hundred times more influential in the lives of the average teenager than the pastor or youth pastor working in the local church.

Make no mistake about it, powerful cultural and educational institutions are working overtime to spoil each successive generation through philosophy and vain deceit. The inability to discern on the part of Christians is due to an overweening enthusiasm for mainstream entertainment and trust in apostate writers, producers and directors. More importantly, the failure to discern is lodged in the abandonment of love for both Christ and His law, on the part of the Christian church.   Christ said, *"If you love me, keep my commandments"* (John 14:15). The Pharisees made the law of God of none effect because their *heart was far from Him* (Matt. 15:6-8).

Story and metaphor will point us to that which is true or false, that which is good or that which is evil. It may blur the lines between good and evil, or it may clearly label evil as good and good as evil. Unless the man of God is firmly grounded in the ethical and epistemological definitions found in God's Word, he most certainly will be spoiled by philosophy and vain deceit. The metaphors that are accepted by a community or nation will either affirm a biblical worldview or a false worldview. Western society proves its apostasy by its cultural incarnations, especially when the Harry Potter and Twilight series lead the way.

10: Worldviews at the Movies

"The demons love the abominations of the stage, which chastity does not love. They love, in the sorceries of the magicians, "a thousand arts of inflicting harm," which innocence does not love. Yet both chastity and innocence, if they wish to obtain anything from the gods, will not be able to do so by their own merits, except their enemies act as mediators on their behalf." (Augustine, The City of God, 8.18)

To ignore the influence of film and television in the war of ideas in the Western world would be akin to ignoring the influence of mosques and madrasas upon Saudi Arabia. The influence is obvious. Listen to conversations in the youth groups of a typical evangelical church, and you will soon learn that the average youth retains more from Saturday night's blockbuster film than he did from the Sunday morning sermon.

Given that the visual medium can be greatly influential and dangerous in the hands of wicked men, it is understandable that some Christians would call into question the morality of the whole field of dramatic arts, theater, and film. And they should be concerned, when the majority of Hollywood directors are professedly non-Christian or anti-Christian. Of the 25 most influential Hollywood directors, 78% are avowed atheists and lapsed Christians, 16% are Catholic, and 8% are Liberal Protestant.[1] When perversions, false worldviews, and idolatry predominate in a society, Christians are more tempted to dispense with all visual metaphor (sculpture, art, etc.). This however is not biblical, first because "all things are lawful, but not all things are expedient" (1 Cor. 6:12, 10:23). Also, remember that Solomon's temple was beautifully decorated with carvings of pomegranates, oxen, lions, cherubim, and palm trees (1 Kings 6). If the Old Testament allowed for liberty in these matters, it certainly follows that the New Testament would not further curtail liberty (Col. 2:15-22).

Although God's Word does command and commend certain art forms, we still should be careful not to overly accentuate their importance.   The modern church leader or lay person places considerable emphasis on music and the visual medium, certainly more of an emphasis than Peter and Paul encouraged in the first century. Music ministry was not a major focus in the early church. The visual medium and music both carry an intensely emotional impact, and therefore manipulate the unsanctified mind and heart. Therefore, immature Christians will want to place too much weight on this media. For example, many hoped that Mel Gibson's *The Passion of the Christ* (2004) would send a sweeping evangelical reformation across the known world. It did not. There are multiple reasons for this, but the key lesson for Christians is found in Romans 10:14. The preaching of the Word is God's assigned means for the conversion of souls. However strongly Christian producers may want to believe that films play a seminal role in establishing a person's adherence to the truth, the Gospel, or the Christian worldview, this simply cannot be the case. While films can strengthen an emotional commitment to a preconceived worldview, it is not the primary means whereby a person is convinced and committed to that worldview (at least for the Christian). It may be hard to believe that Pastor Joe's sermon down at Timbuktu Bible Church can compete with Mel Gibson's latest blockbuster or the Top 40 Hot Hits, Big Time Radio Show, yet that is the way God has ordained it. "For after that in the wisdom of God the world by wisdom knew not God, it pleased God by the foolishness of preaching to save them that believe" (1 Cor. 1:21).

Nonetheless, the prophets would use the dramatic visual medium to convey prophetic warnings of judgment and this should guide our thinking on the use of it. For example, Isaiah walked naked and barefoot for three years (Isa. 20:3-4). Ezekiel acted like an exile

(Ezek. 12:3-6), he shaved his beard and burned part of it (Ezek. 5:1-3), and he built a model city and burned human dung (Ezek. 4:1-12). This all fits into the category of dramatic theater, but the theme of these "productions" was not redemption and their objective was not entertainment. Rather they were metaphors of judgment. Some of the most effective films are those that speak of the inevitable judgment that will come upon the wicked. Conversely, many modern Christians would prefer to use the medium for the redemptive message over against these prophetic warnings.

Too many Christian movie reviews are just too shallow. Counting cuss words and sex scenes may have some value, encouraging a few Christians to dismiss the film entirely. However we cannot stop here. I fear that many believers enter the theater and the world of media as babes in the woods, as children entering a nuclear warzone armed with little pellet guns. They have no idea what is happening to them because they are not prepared to interpret the story on multiple levels.

When a movie production house spends $100 million on a film, the movie will generally involve a multilayered story and will use the brightest minds in the world to direct the production. If the majority of Hollywood producers are atheists and lapsed Christians, by their own profession, you would expect them to lead a Christian apostasy. This will be their trajectory. From the outset then, Christians must be on their guard, careful and discerning. In this chapter, I want to present a method by which to analyze films from various angles and on different levels.

Some Christians have adopted the misconception that what is expertly presented is always good artistic expression. This error underlies much of the Christian liberal arts program in our day. Somehow they forget that the devil is a smooth liar, and he can package his ideas well. They ignore the symbiotic, close weaving of the method and the message and they come to accept the message because they are so enamored by the presentation. When visiting Athens, Paul was taken aback by the sheer number of idols displayed in the city. Though he may have been impressed with the expert carvings done by the Athenian idol designers, he was still certain that they were grotesque idols representing false ideas and abhorrent religions.

In every film or book review, most people want to know if the movie is worth watching or if the literature is worth reading. These are important considerations, but the purpose of this book is not to provide specific recommendations for each and every family. Rather, I will provide a list of analytical devices by which Christian families may judge whether films are worth watching. Suffice it to say for now, that if the film is flawed on fundamental and multiple levels, Christians should be careful not to have fellowship with the unfruitful works of darkness.

FIRST LEVEL: THE GENRE

The first level of analysis takes on the genre itself. The Christian should be aware of the purpose, the theory of reality, or the meta-narrative surrounding the genre in which the story takes place. Take for example, the horror genre, very popular in the theater today. The purpose of the horror film is to illicit dread and fear in the presence of evil. In fact, the very "best" horror films will convince the audience of the ultimate sovereignty of evil. In such films, the evil is not vanquished and cannot be vanquished. In the twelve episodes of *Friday the 13th*, Jason simply cannot die; he comes back to life again and again to murder anybody in his path. Freddy Krueger from *Nightmare on Elm Street* returns to the dream world nine times for more murder and mayhem. Somehow, this disembodied spirit is able to reach from the dream world into the real world to kill without restraint. In the six films produced by the *Child's Play* series, the disembodied spirit of a serial killer inhabits a doll called "Chucky" and continues his evil work. *The Texas Chainsaw Massacre* series (soon to be sixteen films), features the sheriff of the town in cahoots with a murderous family and almost nobody escapes their bloody work. Then the highly successful *Paranormal Activity* series clearly attributes unlimited power and control to demons, allowing for no hope whatsoever through Christian exorcism. These movies are meant to be even more frightening than the original supernatural horror film, *The Exorcist*, in which a demon takes the upper hand over the Roman Catholic "Sons of Sceva Department of Exorcists" (Acts 19:14). Thus evil gradually becomes omnipresent, omniscient, and omnipotent in the minds of those who participate. As the communicant in the theater submits himself to the power of this evil, he responds in "appropriate" fear. Herein lies the danger of the genre. What you fear is what you worship; and who you fear is fundamental to the biblical definition of wisdom. "The fear of the LORD is the beginning of knowledge: but fools despise wisdom and instruction" (Prov. 1:7). The horror genre is especially problematic because the object of fear is something besides God.

> "The fear of man bringeth a snare: but whoso putteth his trust in the LORD shall be safe." (Prov. 29:25)

The ultimate horror of the horror film is what it does to the hearts of those who play with it. If God is not sovereign over the evil actions of men and demons, then evil is sovereign. In this case, all things do not work together for good by the sovereign will of God. By the rationale of these stories, God's right to define good and evil is forfeited, so the distinction between good and evil fades.

Over the last decade, Christians have attempted to produce books and movies in the horror genre as well. By disallowing a Christian view of reality, where God is sovereign over the free actions of men, they unwittingly leave room for the sovereignty of evil and fall into the same trap as the secular moviemakers. According to the rules of the horror genre, we are supposed to get chills up the spine when we read about some fellow taking a Craftsman drill to somebody's foot (as in Ted Dekker's *The Bride Collector*). However, as a Christian writes a story, the reader should tremble to discover that there is a God Who is real, and Who is far more to be feared than some deranged serial killer. This God killed billions of people and animals with a worldwide flood in an act of dreadful judgment on a world of serial killers. This is a God who sends people to hell forever. Now, that's something worth writing about.

At root, the horror genre waters down our sensitivity to the real reality, the real horror, the true horror: the horror of sin, the horror of the cross, and the overwhelming victory achieved over evil.

THE METAPHYSICAL LEVEL

Every storywriter and film producer holds to some worldview. He will commit to that worldview with varying levels of consistency, since consistency is one thing human beings do not do well. Natural man knows the truth of God and suppresses the truth in unrighteousness, according to the Apostle Paul (Rom. 1:18). This does not mean that all movies produced by unbelievers contain zero shades of Christian truth at all. Indeed, there are still vestiges of a thousand years of Christian thinking that seep out of the pores of the Western mind and into artistic expression. Nonetheless, apostasy still predominates and Hollywood is no exception to the rule as the Christian worldview fades to black.

Typically, a film's theory of reality (technically referred to as "the metaphysic") is revealed by the "guru" or "hero" of the story at some point in the movie. It is not hard to find it if you are listening or watching for it. The metaphysic of the story is significant because it provides a foundation for everything else taught in the film. If you find that the filmmakers have gotten the metaphysic wrong, then you will find hardly anything positive to say about the film (just as a Christian believer would not have anything commendable to say about the Islam or Hindu worldview, for example).

Six out of seven of the biggest box office blockbusters of all time are categorized in either the science fiction or superhero genre. The Star Wars franchise holds two positions in the list. In this culture-defining film series, Obi-Wan, the Jedi guru reveals his understanding of the nature of the universe when he says, "The Force is what gives a Jedi his power. It's an energy field created by all living things. It surrounds us and penetrates us. It binds the galaxy together. . ." Later he explains that the evil Darth Vader was "seduced by the dark side of the Force."[2] Thus, we find here the monist metaphysic, in which a single force distributes power to all without distinction. This "force" is confined to the universe, created by the universe itself, and is not to be found outside of it. Thus, the storywriters make no distinction between the Creator and the creature. The Christian worldview differs sharply from this as construed by the first ten words of Genesis:

"In the beginning God created the heaven and the earth." (Gen. 1:1)

The most successful of the films belonging to the $1.5 billion Superman franchise was released in 2013—*Man of Steel*. Of the six releases, this episode provided one of the most explicit statements concerning the metaphysic underlying Superman. The film provides extensive coverage of Superman's origins in Krypton. Though raised by farm parents in Kansas, Superman is the progeny of a dying civilization on the planet Krypton.

There are two basic metaphysical perspectives that play against each other in the film, with one intended to secure ascendance over the other in the mind of the viewer. First, what I'll call the "Kansas" view is offered when young Superman asks his adopted father why God would do such and such. His father ignores the question. It is the "antiquated and unfashionable" Christian worldview concerning some god who used to exist and was supposed to have been in control of the created realm. Mention of God's "providence" is offered by a dumpy, ignorant farm woman who also happens to be the mother of the school bully. Memories concerning the old Christian order are still there, but fast fading.

Among the most obvious and ubiquitous signals of apostasy found in most films today are the loose references to God and His judgments, using words such as "hell," "damn," and "Oh my God." So it makes sense that this film's Kansas metaphysic recognizes God by way of profanity, because that is what Western apostate nations do. They know about God, but they are in process of rejecting Him. They are seriously embittered against the Christian God and use every opportunity to insult His name.

Set against the Kansas worldview is the Krypton metaphysic (which isn't new to the people of the earth, by the way). Certain characters in the story strongly advocate this Krypton metaphysic, which perpetuates the view that man (or the creature) is in control of his own destiny. There can be no ultimately sovereign God in this picture. However, not all are agreed upon which man, or men, or institution, must control reality. For example, Superman's sage, Kryptonite father explains that all babies born in Krypton have been programmed by the state to fulfill a role for the state. This is "Statist Determination." The alternate solution presented in this story is "Self-Determination." We learn early on that Superman's role is to self-determine his own future on earth. His natural father Jor-El explains the purpose for sending his newborn son to earth: "Every person can be a force for good, free to forge his own destiny." This is very different from the Christian view of reality and redemption. In fact, we may recognize this to be the very essence of the Humanist Manifesto I (1933): "Man is at last becoming aware that he alone is responsible for the realization of the world of his dreams, that he has within himself the power for its achievement."[3]

As the story progresses, it should be obvious which theory will win. Even Superman's Kansas father finally affirms the existentialist worldview when he tells his son, "You're not just anyone. One day, you're going to have to make a choice. You have to decide what kind of man you want to grow up to be. Whoever that man is, good character or bad, it's going to change the world." Also, Superman's name is "Kal-El," which is remarkably similar to the Hebrew word for "Voice of God." If the descendants of Krypton are considered gods, then we are back to the polytheism of the Mormons or the pagan world. Jor-El also tells his wife that Superman will "be a god to [the inhabitants of the earth.]"[4] This is reminiscent of the ancient Greek gods. In true form to the old pagan metaphysical perspective, Jor-El lends hope that one day the other members of the human race may achieve this god-status when he says, "You will give the people an ideal to strive towards. They will race behind you, they will stumble, they will fall. But in time, they will join you in the sun. In time, you will help them accomplish wonders."[5]

Some wish to view Superman as a Christ figure, and the conversation with the priest in *Man Of Steel* takes place while Superman stands in front of a picture of "Christ."[6] Does this salvage the film for the Christian audience? Zealous supporters of Hollywood films also like to point out the redemptive element to the story. However, every world religion realizes a problem with the world and then offers a redemptive scheme. Too many Christians naively point to these dubious connections without thinking twice about the worldview foundation which underlies the entire story. After all, didn't Jesus Christ warn that pseudo-Christs would present themselves in the last days? If this "Christ" has the wrong message, the wrong worldview, the wrong nature, the wrong derivation, and the wrong salvation, can we conclude that He may be the wrong Christ—a false Christ (Mark 13:22)? At one time, Christians would think of a false Christ as presenting a false religion. Why should Hollywood get a pass on this?

Postmodern films increasingly celebrate the meaninglessness of life. In the Academy-Award winning film, No Country for Old Men (2007), the serial killer is a nihilist who flips a coin to determine the fate of his victims. He gets away with his crimes in the end. There Must Be Blood (2007), was another major Academy Award winner (and Best Film of the Decade on various lists), in which another murderer gets away with his crime and the Christian faith is presented as empty and powerless against the bleakness of postmodern nihilism. Another recent film, The Grey (2011), presents the hero bravely fighting nature: a pack of wolves. Throughout the film, there is a little discussion among the protoganists about the existence of God or the effectiveness of prayer. All of this is thrown out the window towards the end of the film. As the hero, Ottway takes on the wolves for the last time, he screams, "Forget faith! Prove yourself! Once more into the fray. Into the last good fight I'll ever know."[7]

The Lion King (1994) was the most popular children's movie (and animated film) of all time, grossing almost $1 billion in worldwide box office receipts. The metaphysic of this movie was not hard to miss when the erudite Mufasa tells young Simba, "Everything you see exists together in a delicate balance...when we die our bodies become the grass, and the antelope eat the grass. And so we are all connected in the great Circle of Life."[8] This is a monist worldview: all humans, animals, and inanimate objects make up a single whole. There is no difference between the Creator and the creature, and there is no afterlife for man. This theory became the basis for the powerful, modern environmentalist movement and for the earth-worship cult. Many Christian families do not see how a movie like this can be harmful, even though the worldview of the youth is rapidly changing from Christian to pagan. According to a recent survey, Millennials are almost three times more likely to believe in a "universal spiritual force" and participate in yoga as a spiritual practice than the Silent Generation.[9]

METAPHYSIC ANALYSIS OF THE GIVER

Capturing rave reviews from the Christian film-rating organizations, the 2014 release The Giver attracted a strong conservative Christian audience. Again, the complete absence of profanity and intimate scenes seem to make for a movie worth recommending in the minds of many Christians. Twice, the film features a family singing the Christmas Carol "Silent Night" for a few brief seconds. These are only ever-so-slight nods to a Christian heritage residing somewhere in the dim past. But what does it matter if the film avoids profanity, while maintaining an underlying worldview that counters Christ?

I noticed while viewing the film that the worldview would surface via particularly poignant statements in the dialogue. Such statements require long and careful reflection, but the average person is not going to stop the film and reflect upon the worldview communicated through the words just spoken. As I would reflect upon some of the more important dialogue, I noticed that I would miss subsequent scenes. These worldviews are not immediately understood or countered in the minds of the viewers. Still, they must seep into the consciousness.

Based on a book for youth, The Giver is a futuristic tale of a highly-regulated, highly-structured totalitarian world that intends to rid the world of evil (by chemical injections and statist regulation). Evil is blamed on human emotion and wrong environmental influence (vs. sin against the law of God). The film rightly condemns the draconian, family-disintegrating Platonic state where "no parent shall know his child, and no child shall know his parent." The state educates, assigns children to homes, determines each person's calling, cares for the elderly, and aborts and euthanizes at will. There are no true families, no family economies, and no free enterprise. For many of us, it is eerily familiar to what we find in the modern secular state.

At one point in the story, the proto-antagonist gets it right when she says, "Man always makes the wrong choice." She forgets however, that she is of the same human race, even as she represents the state. She is part of the problem, and therefore cannot provide the solution. Two forms of salvation are presented in the film, both of which do not properly address man's basic problem or the necessary transcendent (God-sourced) solution. On the one hand, the antagonists offer an ineffectual salvation by the state, so the hero presents another salvation plan by the restoration of human emotion. When one character in the film kills a baby (via a clinical procedure), the murder is rightly presented as a shocking, dastardly action. However, we must ask the all-important question, "Why? Why is this immoral?" As the screenwriter explains it to us, the restrictions placed on human emotion rendered the man incapable of loving the child. Consequently, the murder is blamed upon the statist programming. Of course, the same human emotion that can bring about a phileo-love can produce selfishness, hatred, and murder. The authors forget to inform us of this small catch. Merely restoring a man's emotions and free will cannot save him. By the end of the film, the bottom-line message comes across loud and clear: a world filled with love and hate, hugs and murder, and polytheism is better than a world without emotion. While a secular audience may accept that, Christians are horrified by these equally evil alternatives. The ungodly cannot find a middle way between the unity and the particulars. They will forever revert between statist autonomy and personal autonomy as the only possible salvation schemes for man. Nonetheless, we can be sure that only the Lord Jesus Christ can save us from the horns of this dilemma.

11: The Ethical Level

Discerning Good and Evil in the Movies

Most stories play out on various ethical levels. There is the ethic that drives the main story line, and then there are the subplots, the character development, and the tertiary ethical matters. If there is a fundamental ethical flaw in the system, God's law should identify it. All worldviews maintain some ethical standard, and some may even occasionally conform to God's law at points. For example, cannibals may actually maintain certain standards of decency and honor within their own communities. They may insist that their children chew human flesh with their mouths closed as a matter of decorum. Likewise, the Hollywood social context does retain some sort of ethical standard. However, endorsing a film on the basis of a few tertiary elements in the ethical construct (e.g. table manners) while minimizing the more fundamental problems (e.g. cannibalism), is a classic example of straining at gnats and swallowing camels (Matt. 23:24). This is not uncommon for some "Christian" film reviews as well.

When the heroes or heroines are vampires, witches, homosexuals, or bank robbers, it is hard to commend them even when they save the "damsel in distress." This applies to the Harry Potter series previously mentioned. Yet another popular series offers one more illustration of this. *The Hunger Games: Catching Fire* (2013) was the most popular movie of the year according to BoxOfficeMojo.com. Author of the story, Suzanne Collins, joins J. K. Rowling (author of the Harry Potter Series) and Stephanie Meyer (author of the Twilight series), to compose the trio of the most popular authors of our century. *The*

Hunger Games story introduces a complicated ethical conundrum for modern teens in which a teenage girl is forced into a kill-or-be-killed gladiatorial combat. The heroine first offers herself in the place of her sister, who had been selected to engage in competitions similar to the old Roman gladiatorial games. Twice, the heroine enters the field and kills other young people forced into the same competition.

While Scripture does allow some violence for the sake of self preservation, the preservation of the lives of others is a higher value. Therefore, we find Abraham defending the life of Lot and his family against the marauders. We find Moses defending the life of a fellow Israelite, and we find Christ giving up His life for His friends. In the Hunger Games scenario, two deleterious and tyrannical conditions are placed upon the combatants simultaneously. First, the civil magistrate has deputized a citizen to kill other innocent citizens, none of whom have been convicted of a crime. Secondly, the civil magistrate has deputized others to kill this same citizen. Now, what is the proper ethical response to this? First, the Christian must never murder innocent human beings, even though the magistrate may require it of him or her. The Hebrew midwives in Exodus 1:14-22 serve as our example here. It is clearly testified of them in the historical record that these women feared God more than they feared the king, and they are commended for it. Second, the Christian may not kill the deputized magistrate, although she may attempt to flee in order to protect her own life. David serves as a good example in this scenario. On more than one occasion, he had the opportunity to kill Saul and his deputies as they hunted him down, yet he refused to "touch the Lord's anointed" (1 Sam. 24:1-10).

In these situational ethics conundrums, the underlying assumption is that there is no God who can provide a way of escape for the Christian. God is clearly left out of the metaphysic. Outside of the fact that the heroine, Katniss, takes God's name in vain (and she does this more often than any other character in the film), there is no recognition of God in the world of the Hunger Games. If God is not sovereign over the evil in this world, man and woman are left to fend for themselves. The assumed metaphysic becomes that the deterministic world of the fates as is offered in the classical humanist world. If man is subjected to fatalism, human responsibility to ethical standards entirely dissolves. Any Christian familiar with pagan philosophy understands this game and the evil of it.

While it is true that Katniss shows sacrificial love for her sister and has a kind word here and there for another combatant, the overarching theme of the story is her participation in the gladiatorial killing games. Regrettably, there was very little uproar from the Christian church regarding the shocking violence contained in these films. Where was Telemachus, the monk who put an end to the Roman games in 404 A.D.? Any Christian should do what Telemachus did. He jumped into the amphitheater and commanded the crowd in the name of the risen Christ to stop the madness. Although the humble monk was killed for his trouble, the crowd quickly dissipated and the killing games abated soon afterwards.

On the release of the first *Hunger Games* movie, protest from Christian leaders was almost non-existent. There was little discussion about Saul and David or the Hebrew midwives. There wasn't much said about biblical definitions for interposition, in which an alternate magistrate may defend the citizenry against a tyrannical magistrate. These are important matters for the future of Christian civilization. Without God's laws, we are left with tyranny and revolutionary anarchy where human society is caught in a deadly, bloody, horrific scenario, not unlike *The Hunger Games*. If Christian pastors were well-versed in God's laws, and would hold to them with strong conviction, there may be some hope for preserving human life in the future.

When God's laws are ignored, however, all things are permissible (to paraphrase Fyodor Dostoyevsky's famous remark). Recently, a Christian legal defense organization put its resources towards defending transvestites who wish to cross dress in American public high schools.[1] Another Christian pastor defended incestuous marriages in a recently published book.[2] Antinomian Christianity is only contributing to the cultural demise of the Western world. Moreover, the consequences of these subtle messages on the hearts and minds of a hundred million children watching these movies and reading these books will be devastating. As they watch Katniss follow the plan and kill other young people in this "game," these young women and men are being prepared to submit to the tyrannical and vicious systems of government that may very well return to a pagan, anti-Christian world.

Countless foul men and women are presented as heroes in Hollywood films. Almost every hero or heroine in Hollywood movies breaks the third and seventh commandments with impunity. They routinely commit fornication, adultery, and homosexual acts, while they are generally considered virtuous for it. Historically, the English spy James Bond commits fornication as part of the job, while he saves the world from mass-murderers or would-be terrorists. Occasionally he kills for personal vengeance, thus becoming a murderer himself. The message comes across loud and clear: Adultery, fornication, and an occasional murder are fine as long as you are saving the world from other murderers. *Titanic* (1997) is the second most popular movie of all time, and the glorification of fornication is a primary theme. The producers seemed to miss the theme of God's judgment upon human pride, represented in the real story. In this modern retelling of the story, the main character, Jack draws pornographic material and fornicates with Rose on a lower deck before the ship goes down. Of course, all of this was counter to the wishes of Rose's mother. Their fornication is essential to their love story, and seventy-five years later the old woman still says that "Jack saved me in every way that a person could be saved."[3] That is the saddest testimony of all. Where there is no repentance or remorse, where there are no clear consequences for wicked actions, and where there is only commendation for that sinful behavior, the film sets itself in rebellion to God. This is an example of how modern storytelling sets out to call evil good, and good evil (Isa. 5:20).

THE ETHICS OF HUMOR

There are two forms of humor, namely attack humor and endearing humor. This distinction provides a strong ethical component to comedy. As Christians, we must attack or oppose that which is evil and endear that which is good.

Throughout Scripture, you will find several instances where humor is employed—mostly in the form of attack. We do not find Jesus opening up His sermons with a few jokes, and one would look far and wide for the use of humor in the epistles. An excessive use of humor is a strong indication that we have little sobriety, sincerity, and maturity in our present society. Where men are given to unrestrained humor and laughter, there is no doubt a severe deficiency of the fear of God to be found.

Nonetheless, Elijah uses mockery or satire to illustrate the futility of pagan worship on Mount Carmel (1 Kings 18:27). Our Lord caricatures the Pharisees as those that strain at gnats and swallow camels (Matt. 23:24). And Ezekiel describes the spiritual harlotry of Israel, using the strongest satirical language possible (Ezek. 23:20ff). All in all, the Bible makes sparse use of these humorous forms. When a ministry is consumed with satire, three problems emerge. First, there is something of a net loss of the fear of God that results. The impression given to the modern world is that the ministry is not serious about its satire. So the satire becomes more of a show. Secondly, there is no resolution in the Gospel of Christ. Satire attacks, but where is the grace? Where is the hope of mercy in Christ? Then, there is the impression that the satirists are proud and have no sins to confess for themselves. Humor therefore, must be handled with much wisdom—even more wisdom than other forms of communication. A two-year old has no business handling a chainsaw. As it turns out, young men and women are not careful in their use of humor.

One of the favorite lines used by popular "clean" comedians makes for a good illustration of how worldview impacts comedy. It goes something like this. First, he informs the audience that he and his wife have stopped spanking their children, all in the pretense of taking the "higher moral ground." Then he says, "We taze them instead." The audience erupts in loud laughter on the punchline. But now, the discerning Christian stops for a moment and examines the worldview behind the line. Is the comedian treating the matter of spanking or tazing children with endearment or mockery? Is he endearing his audience to child abuse, or is he attacking child abuse?

Of course, the answer is neither. He refuses to commit one way or the other. The audience laughs at the unexpected comeback, but they do not much consider the worldview behind it. What is chilling about these comedy shows is that they both further establish and reveal a worldview of post-modern relativism in the minds of the participants. It is the refusal to commit to either good or evil that makes for post-modern humor.

REDEMPTION

Almost every story includes something about redemption, since every worldview defines man's problem and suggests a solution. However, a film or book is propaganda for a false religion when it gets the problem wrong and presents the wrong solution. This is something that most Christians are not considering if they are still watching Hollywood movies. They would sooner walk into a theater than they would walk into a mosque or hear a lecture on eastern meditation. Why Christians are naive in the theater must have something to do with the fact that they have not paid attention to the teachings in their Christian churches for the last ten, twenty, or thirty years.

The Dead Poets Society (1989) has Robin Williams playing a literature professor who gets the metaphysic wrong, suggesting that his students are nothing but worm food: cosmic dust in a purposeless universe. Hence, the moral of the story follows the Roman Horace's advice: "Seize the day, trusting as little as possible in the future." The professor encourages his students to think and act independently of all social norms, let alone biblical norms. The students comply with his advice and find their redemption in disobeying authorities (parents included), sharing pornographic material, and generally casting off all moral and social restraints. Assuming that the lead actor was committed to the worldview he propounded in the film, it came as no surprise that he committed suicide on August 11th, 2014.

The existentialist worldview is probably the most common worldview operating in Pop culture today. At the outset, the existentialist admits that the universe has no meaning. Hollywood loves to present men like Forrest Gump, who appear on the screen with a "sense of disorientation and confusion in the face of an apparently meaningless or absurd world."[4] Man is left to define himself and to act authentically (by Sartre's perfect ideal of autonomy) so as to define his own existence and establish his own value. Redemption for the existentialist comes when the hero learns to follow his heart (as in *A Time to Kill, Meet Joe Black, The Mask of Zorro, Mulan, Hercules, Romancing the Stone, Ferris Bueller's Day Off, What About Bob?, Legends of the Fall,* and *The Bridges of Madison County*), control his own destiny (*The Truman Show*), improve his self-perception (*Toy Story*), decide for himself to commit fornication and to reject traditional morality (*Pleasantville*), or assume responsibility and claim moral rectitude for the most immoral things he had done, including murder (*Crimes and Misdemeanors*).[5]

The existentialist hangs on to the thinnest thread, hoping he can somehow establish meaning, purpose and essence for life by his own self-determined actions. However, the "feel good" films we watch are only a cheap sales job. Perhaps they will delay suicide for a few days or years. The redemption offered by the existentialist proves to be wholly inadequate in the end.

PORTRAYING EVIL

Nothing in life should be attempted in the absence of wisdom, and portraying evil in film is no exception to that rule. The Bible is filled with horrific stories, including the story of the adultery of David and Bathsheba and the tale of the concubine at Gibeah (Judg. 19). Arguably, there has never been a more evil story than this in the history of man. It is an honest portrayal of the moral bankruptcy of Israel in the years of the Judges. But how is evil like this to be portrayed on the movie screen? Here are several guidelines for the depiction of evil in script and film.

1. "Have no fellowship with the unfruitful works of darkness" (Eph. 5:11). It is one thing to make note of the sin of cannibalism, and it is quite another to sit down at dinner with Hannibal the Cannibal, who was featured in a film series that grossed just under $1 billion in worldwide box office sales. With each successive film

in the franchise, the audience is treated to increasingly more explicit details about Hannibal's tortures, murders, and cannibalistic habits. Screenwriter Ted Tally explains the thoughts behind these products: "People respond to him. They find him seductive. I think there's a part of all of us that likes watching an anti-hero, someone who can get away with doing and saying things we could never get away with."[6] Call it "morbid curiosity" or "edgy voyeurism," but the root of it all is found in man's sinful nature. There is a part of us that is seduced by pure, unadulterated evil, which we Christians call "the flesh." The fleshy heart needs little encouragement to perform ungodly, perverted acts. If the human heart is depraved, deceitful above all things, and desperately wicked (Jer. 17:9), then one can hardly imagine the ungodly effects of expertly produced films like these. As the viewer is invited to sit at the table with Hannibal, he enters fellowship (*koinonia* in Greek) with the unfruitful works of darkness. According to 1 Corinthians 10:19-21, people sometimes actually fellowship with demons if they participate in the demons' ceremonies and rituals, including those conducted in Hollywood films.

2. When the Christian is confronted with the unfruitful works of darkness, he has one responsibility as required in the second half of the verse (Eph. 5:11). Reprove the evildoers. Preach against the evil. Loudly protest it. Instead of speaking of those things that are done in secret (Eph. 5:12), we shine the light of God's standards of righteousness upon them. We cannot permit a moment of autonomy in which the flesh pretends that there is something to approve, something to meditate upon, something to study in these evil works. Philippians 4:8 instructs us to meditate or focus upon things that are honest, true, lovely, just, and virtuous. The Greek word used in the phrase "think on these things" is *logizomai*, a word that denotes lengthy contemplation and meditation. Whereas we might for a brief moment think about a sin mentioned in Leviticus 18 or Leviticus 20, we are not to focus upon it. Thankfully, God's Word also quickly resolves the sin in the condemnation or the civil penalty assigned to it (in these references).

Herein lies the problem with the "nude" scene in which an actor is subjected to shame before the viewing audience. For the sake of definition, the Bible defines nakedness minimally as the display of the buttocks in 2 Samuel 10:4-5. So if a lady guest at a dinner party accidentally catches her dress and reveals her private areas to the rest of the guests, the proper response is either to turn faces away or throw a cloth over the poor lady who is subjected to the embarrassment. Most brothers would helpfully cover their sister's nakedness in such a situation. This is why Leviticus 18 speaks of incest as an "uncovering" of a family member's nakedness. When viewing a film, or a billboard on the highway, in which a woman's nakedness is uncovered, the only two proper responses will be to: (1). cover your eyes, or (2). cover the movie screen or billboard with something appropriate. Also, public display of generic nude bodies of females or males casts shame on females or males in general. If the media guy was to flash cartoon nude bodies of women on the power point screen on a Sunday morning, every brother in the congregation should avert his eyes and attempt to cover the nakedness for the shame it brings to sisters in general.

Film producers and directors have a responsibility to God for their portrayal of evil. If they lure the audience into taking the side of the bank robber to the point that the audience is hoping he will get away with it in the end, these cultural leaders have set themselves against God and His law. If they pit one wicked man against another wicked man in order to excuse one preferred form of sin, they are advocating more autonomy. Unbelieving writers are often adept in their descriptions of human nature, but most of the time they hardly condemn it or redeem it, either way.

Presentation of evil in film is difficult, for the very reason that it invites emotional connection in almost every frame. To read of cannibalism is one thing (as we read of it in the Bible), but to watch somebody cutting off a human arm and preparing it for human consumption in the kitchen is quite another matter. Film is explicit because it is a visual medium. Fellowship comes too easily. Thus, the best directors will leave much of the evil in the story to innuendo, or leave it off stage.[7]

Is there any point at which an actor in a movie is permitted to take God's name in vain? Or is it ever appropriate for any character in a story to use perverse language? It is true that Sennacherib and Rabshakeh are quoted directly as they taunt Israel and Jehovah God at the walls of Jerusalem (Isa. 36). Biblical accounts like this must allow for the inclusion of certain blasphemous words in a story, so long as they are contained within quotation marks of some form. This is easier said than done, especially when it comes to film. For example, an actor may pretend to rob a bank, but it is not so easy to "pretend to be naked" if the actor is really baring his backside in a scene depicting sexuality. The question concerning profanity is more difficult, partially because it is hard to put words within a movie *in quotes*. Also, the goal of modern acting is stark realism where nothing is *in quotes*. The actions are meant to look realistic, and the profanity is supposed to feel realistic as well. How does one fear God while taking His name in vain on set? And how is this best conveyed to the audience? While I cannot say that this would be impossible to do, I still cannot come up with a scenario in which it could be done rightly. For most Hollywood movies, it is the hero who takes God's name in vain and he is meant to sound cool while he is doing it. In fact, swearing with impunity is one of the highest forms of "cool" in our day. Christians should outright repudiate this form of profanity.

Modern films work hard for a realistic presentation, and thus actors are expected to play the part by portraying evil as realistically as possible. The audience must at least momentarily forget that they are experiencing metaphor. They are supposed to believe that the man on the screen is really as evil as he presents himself to be.

Christian filmmakers should be comfortable with portraying evil off-screen. I would also suggest using certain agreed upon melodramatic affectations that keep the evil words and actions within quotation marks. The form chosen must not minimize the nature of evil, or allow for the approval of it in its presentation.

THE MAN IN THE IRON CAGE

Popular culture is popular because the public identifies with the ideas and sentiments presented therein. Generally, cultural arts are more descriptive than prescriptive. Poems, songs, and books "describe" more than they "prescribe." Therefore, culture lauds the best descriptions in form and substance. If they describe human nature or human behavior with any accuracy, such that the market identifies with the description, the artistic work will typically do well.

For the Christian, however, mere description is not sufficient to call an artistic form a good work. An artist may describe a fallen, sinful world, but we should be concerned about the manner in which it is presented. Does the artist accept the fallen state as inevitable, inescapable, or even preferable? After the aesthetic experience is over, have the participants surrendered themselves to the conditions expressed in the medium?

Roger Miller's song "Dang Me" reached the top position on Billboard's Country Charts in 1964, and it won the Grammy award for the Best Country Western Song the same year.[8] Written by Miller himself in the first person ("I," "me") the song tells the story of a man who frequents the bar scene and spends his family's grocery money, while his wife is taking care of a baby at home. The man is a loser and he's happy to be a loser, so "damn me," he says. On one hand, the song provides a sad but accurate description of the hopelessly irresponsible father and husband of the last century or two. But does an accurate description of a drunk legitimize a song like this, or render it edifying?

The words of this song will send a chill up the spine of anybody who understands what the songwriter means. Yet is that what the songwriter is trying to achieve? Does he want us to condemn the man or shudder for his soul? Why should we appreciate this song? Was the songwriter's goal to get every loser father in America to buy the album and bebop to it? The song reportedly contains "lighthearted humor" from a songwriter known to have had problems with depression, drug addiction, and multiple divorces.[9] The popularity of songs such as this one explains why the majority of households are led by single women and divorcees. The operative word is "hopeless." If we can't fight them, we join them—or at least we laugh at them.

Roger Miller's loser father reflects the picture of John Bunyan's "Man in the Iron Cage" presented in *The Pilgrim's Progress*. This reprobate in a cage produces millions of popular songs, and he seems to attract quite a following. Of course, he has lost all hope of redemption, so he just makes himself comfortable and cranks out the songs. How are we supposed to feel for the drunk "wasting away again in Margaritaville" even though it is "his own damned fault?" Are we supposed to enjoy the iron cage constructed by Jimmie Buffet? Have the musician and his fans resigned themselves to the inevitability of damnation? These are questions hardly ever asked by the listeners of Top 40 stations. Occasionally, popular music will warn of the negative consequences of excessive drinking and drugs, but their reasoning is usually confined to personal health concerns. In the "No No Song," Hoyt Axton is just plain old tired of "waking up on the floor." In "Sunday Morning Coming Down," Kris Kristofferson is still wishing he were stoned, because "there's something in a Sunday that makes a body feel alone." The song depicts the apostate who retains a faint memory of what a Christian church service is, but would prefer sleeping on city sidewalks to genuine repentance. What sort of person might relate to this song? Obviously, a Christian can hardly spend much time with the man in the iron cage, let alone climb into the cage for extended fellowship. 2 Corinthians 6:14-17 is usually applied to unequally yoked marriages, but it actually speaks more broadly to any unequal fellowship:

> "Be ye not unequally yoked together with unbelievers: for what fellowship hath righteousness with unrighteousness? And what communion hath light with darkness? And what concord hath Christ with Belial? Or what part hath he that believeth with an infidel? And what agreement hath the temple of God with idols? For ye are the temple of the living God; as God hath said, 'I will dwell in them, and walk in them; and I will be their God, and they shall be My people. Wherefore come out from among them, and be ye separate,' saith the Lord, 'and touch not the unclean thing; and I will receive you.'" (2 Cor. 6:14-17)

THE META-ETHIC

The discerning Christian should also consider the meta-ethic: the basic ethical principle whereby the characters in a story make moral decisions. The meta-ethic may be the most insidious message in modern storytelling because it lies so far beneath the surface. An example of this is the modern thriller or spy story, in which the highest value is the survival of the empire or the national order. For example, in one recent blockbuster, *National Treasure*, the hero steals the United States Declaration of Independence from the National Archives. He then defaces the document. But it is all fine because the ancient document was about to be stolen by somebody else anyway; and besides, he was searching for a treasure of much higher value than the Declaration of Independence. To make matters worse, the hero of the story steals the treasure from a church property, then turns it over to the government because it "belongs to the people." This film deftly lures us into admiring the hero's choices, because the ends justify the means. Yet after a while the value of the end result dissipates, leaving "the means" as the only important value. This philosophical meta-ethic is known as "pragmatism."

Pragmatism allows for all possible violations of God's laws to be legitimized so long as the hero accomplishes his goals. The Christian reader may recognize this ethical approach in the story of Uzzah in the Old Testament (2 Sam. 6:3-8). This man jumped in to save the ark of the covenant as it was about to tip off an ox-drawn cart. God killed him for his trouble. Because Uzzah was more committed to preventing something potentially bad from happening, he was pressed to break God's laws in the process. Uzzah was the prototype pragmatist.

Many "conservative" Christians were particularly thrilled in 2010 when Jack Bauer of the television series *24* tortured his victims with knives, pliers, acid, and blow torches to get the answers he wanted from his antagonists. Sometimes he would do it for private revenge, and sometimes he was trying to save a toppling empire from nuclear annihilation.[10] Since the days of the James Bond novels and films, national spies have been permitted to operate above the law of God and the law of the land. Hollywood films and television production companies are not thinking in terms of biblical law, although there are plenty of lawful means that could be used to save the life of a president or to protect people from terrorists.

THE SOCIAL LEVEL

Tied in somewhat closely to ethical analysis is the social analysis. The discerning Christian must think about the social context in which the story takes place. A Christian social system is based in the covenantal, relational world of family and church, while the anti-Christian world of Cain is the world of the vagabond. He excommunicates himself by disfellowshipping himself from family and church. This was the vision of the humanist world of Plato's *The Republic*, in which the man and the woman "guardians" come together for only a temporary liaison to bear children. Writes Plato in Book Five, "No son shall know his father. No father shall know his son." This is essential for the humanist. The political state is of essence and the family is negligible. Thus, it is important to the humanist that James Bond does not know his father, and that Jason Bourne has no connection to family whatsoever. When hundreds of millions of children watched *Mr. Roger's Neighborhood* and *Sesame Street* during the 1970s, 1980s, and 1990s, few parents thought about the social context. Who is Mr. Rogers? Where is his wife? Where are his children? And who is Oscar's father? Are Ernie and Bert brothers or homosexuals? Why are the relationships formed around a socialist community, rather than within the covenantal structures of families and churches? This is how powerful media forces redesign human society while few families really pay much attention to it.

A fundamental cause for the dystopia found in the wildly popular *The Hunger Games* is the failure of fatherhood. Throughout the films, there are no godly fathers, pastors, or sheriffs to be found. There are no families or churches of any relevance. Actually, there is one grandfather presented, but trouble is, he's the arch villain. His granddaughter appears well-balanced, and their relationship still appears intact. While there are men shuffling about in the story, they are unimportant to the story. This is the dystopia. Without fathers, this world holds no possibility of political freedom and no hope for social reconstruction. When a society loses its fathers, families, and churches, there is no way that a teenage girl with a bow and arrow and an acumen for killing citizens in gladiatorial combat will ever salvage a civilization. Again, stories like this eerily reflect our present social disintegration. 64% of millennial women have children outside of wedlock,[11] and the largest socialist voting block in America is single women.[12] Tens of millions of teenage girls watch the film and envision themselves in a similar story. Meanwhile, their fathers watch their sports games while "Rome" burns to the ground. This *Hunger Games* world searches in vain for solutions, because it fails to admit the failure of an entire social system.

THE METHODOLOGICAL LEVEL

Worldviews are conveyed, however discretely through the arrangement of scenes, videography, lighting, sound, and music as well. This is the most difficult to analyze, and scarcely one in a thousand would catch the nuances. Setting a current film side by side with one produced in the 1950s would quickly demonstrate stark differences. The 2013 blockbuster *Man of Steel* was mainstream, highly popular, and hardly an avant garde production. However, this was a very different film than those I had watched in the 1980s and 1990s. I couldn't help but notice that the scenes were highly disconnected and fragmented; there appeared to be little or no connection between many of the scenes. The story moved from one location to another without much of an identifiable purpose. When unity is lost in particulars, meaning fades as well. Here is another indication that modern man has abandoned a Christian Trinitarian metaphysic: the storytelling method is descending into postmodern meaninglessness. The agenda comes across in an underhanded way. Are the viewers aware of what is happening to them as they are taken from one scene to the next? Worldviews are caught more than taught.

Symbols chosen by the writers and directors are important as well. Effective directors are efficient in their use of imagery, props, and scenery; almost every element of every scene must contribute something to the story. For six thousand years, dragons signified the devil or evil, and when heroes befriend dragons we should be suspicious of them as in *How to Train Your Dragon* (2010). The cross on the neck of the hotel manager who attempted the mass rescue in *Hotel Rwanda* (2004) spoke volumes, as did the failure of the United Nations officials to rescue anyone. When Spider-Man peeled off his evil, fleshy exterior in the sanctuary of a Christian church in *Spider Man 3* (2007), the symbolism was inescapable to the Christian mind. Of all of the superhero films, this one may have come the closest to a Christian metaphysic.

The casting of a homosexual as the lead actor in a film about missionaries, *End of the Spear* (2005), communicated another message loud and clear. The clash of values was hard to miss, as homosexuals cannot play the part of Christian missionaries or Christian fathers in a believable way. Are Christian filmmakers incapable of telling the difference between a Christian martyr and Nero (the homosexual Caesar who first popularized homosexual marriage)?

SUB-LEVELS: PLOTS AND SUB-THEMES

Most worldviews attempt to identify man's basic problem and then provide a redemptive plan or story. As touched upon earlier, in the case of *Man of Steel*, statism is the initial problem presented. Over the centuries, the planet Krypton replaced natural child birth with state-programmed reproductive systems. Superman's enemy is state-programmed and state-determined to defend the old Kryptonite order. Therefore, the basic problem in the universe is understood to be whatever destroyed Krypton. While we would agree that Krypton's tyrannical system is unethical and evil, from a biblical perspective, man's basic problem is not statist tyranny. It is his broken relationship with God, his insistence upon being "God" and determining his own future, and his determining of his own ethics or standard of goodness apart from God. Somewhere in the film, the bad guys do mention that Kryptonites are higher creatures on the evolutionary scale of things. Superman himself doesn't present any real answer to the evolutionary argument except to add that the Kryptonites destroyed their own planet and thereby proved themselves incapable in the evolution game. The solution for Jor-El is that each individual man determines his own destiny. Polytheism is preferred to statism. Therefore, this movie identifies one problem correctly, but fails to get to the root issue. The solution suggested is as bad as the original problem.

Early in the film, Superman presents himself as a self-sacrificing, magnanimous chap when he dives into a river to save the school bully. He goes to great lengths to protect and honor his mother in a rather punctuated scene in the film. Also, somewhere in the film, the bad guys remind Superman that because he maintains a sense of morality and they do not, they get the edge in the battle.

Sub-themes and sub-plots may produce helpful lessons or hurtful. There is a brief scene in the movie where Superman enters a church and stands next to a picture of Christ. Again, we ask ourselves, "Which Christ?" Is this a positive or negative reference to the true Christ of Scripture? Does Superman replace the true Christ or a false Christ? The stereotypical effeminate priest tells him to save the world, and Superman points out that the world does not deserve to be saved. The priest defines himself as a Kierkegaardian existentialist when he encourages Superman to the irrational "leap of faith." I wonder how many Christian viewers picked that up. It is not uncommon to find a variety of worldviews, a mishmash of gods from the pantheon scattered throughout these films. What is harder to find is a true Christian metaphysic and Christian meta-ethic.

The outrageously popular Disney film, *Frozen* (2013)[13] attracted attention from liberals and conservatives alike for its "progressive agenda."[14] However brief the references to homosexuality and bestiality, the progressives at Disney know what they are doing. Shortly after releasing the film, the Disney Corporation withdrew support from the Boy Scouts when that organization refused to approve homosexual scout leaders[15] (even though the Scouts did open the doors to homosexual scouts as of January 1, 2014). The light, humorous reference to bestiality in the trolls' song would have been easy to miss, and an ambivalent scene referencing something that looked to many to be a homosexual family is passed off as unimportant. But, how else would progressives introduce such subjects to 5-year-old children from Christian homes? Disney producers may be radical progressives, but they're not stupid. We've come a long way from Snow White and the Seven Dwarfs. It doesn't take a PhD in cultural studies to recognize the homosexual motto "Born This Way" in the dialogue from *Frozen*. Anybody living in the 21st Century Western world would see the connection with Lady Gaga's pro-homosexual hit song *Born This Way*. Hans Christian Andersen would have hardly recognized his story.

Yet, I'm sure that these critiques come off as puritan quibbling and nit-picky to many families who enjoy these films. After all, how could ten seconds of tertiary content in a movie possibly corrupt an otherwise wonderful story? How might a single paint stroke across the Mona Lisa's upper lip possibly ruin an otherwise masterful work of art? Some Christian parents might be bothered by a ten second nude scene dropped into a Veggie Tales feature, but why would they accept references to unnatural relations with reindeer in a Disney film? What they fail to realize is that all of these cultural experiences make up the narrative of a child's life.

RATING FILMS

If no human being has achieved sinless perfection, is it fair to say that all human creations, metaphors, stories, and symbols will bear flaws as well? Given that we live in an imperfect world, the words of Christ in Matthew 7:1-3 apply:

> *"Judge not, that ye be not judged. For with what judgment ye judge, ye shall be judged: and with what measure ye mete, it shall be measured to you again."*

Of course, this does not preclude all judgments (John 7:24, 2 Cor. 10:4-7). But this does moderate our judgment somewhat. We cannot expect perfection in human creations, yet we are called to make righteous judgments.

Rating systems for films will be somewhat subjective. I recommend a rating system that addresses the practical question, "Is it worth watching?" Some films are not worth watching, some are worth watching once, and some may be worth watching multiple times. In my experience, most of the films I have reviewed are not worth watching. I can't say that for every film, however. There are some films I believe to be suitable and edifying for most audiences. In the case of other films, it would only take five minutes before the discerning viewer decides it is spiritually, morally, intellectually unprofitable—a counterproductive use of time.

However, some films are far more difficult to analyze than others. For example, *Sling Blade* (1996) is a complex film and more difficult to assess. The mentally deficient hero in the story (played by Billy Bob Thornton) is pro-life and he carries a Bible. Carl sincerely wants to protect a young boy from imminent harm at the hands of his mother's boyfriend. The antagonist is presented as an atheist and a drunken, violent man. However, we are left with serious questions after watching this unquestionably disturbing film. Given that the homosexual in the story provides safe haven for the little boy, may we conclude that the film approves of homosexuality? Yet Carl doesn't hesitate to point out that the Bible prohibits a man lying with a man. In the end, the mentally-deficient protagonist is forced to kill the violent man. Could he have avoided the killing, or are we to assume that his mental incapacity exempts him of any guilt? The film is filled with ugly profanities, hopeless conditions, and descriptions of the most dysfunctional and sinful lifestyles. The larger metaphysical perspective in *Sling Blade* still seems to be the same as *Forrest Gump* (1994), where a mentally challenged hero is caught in the vortex of a confused, absurd world. Poor Carl tries to make sense out of it himself, and finds redemption in his own self-determined actions. In the end he feels no guilt for the murders he committed, but instead justifies them. He bluntly states, "I'd reckon I would" do it over again "if I had the chance." The minor theme of compassion for young children and the mild condemnation of homosexuality are commendable, but they cannot overcome the underlying message of ethical autonomy and confusion.

Christians ought not to be bamboozled by artful and thoughtful film productions of the highest order when they originate from the minds of men and women who do not share their worldview. Careful analysis and critique at every level is in order, especially when the world is deceived by these films and young people raised in Christian homes are so easily captured by them. A careful worldview analysis strips away the mystique and rips down the imaginations and every high thing that exalts itself against the knowledge of God (2 Cor. 10:5). These are powerful systems, but they can be dismantled by hearts and minds that are sanctified by the Word and Spirit. Clearly, this work is not for everyone, and of course it must be done with much fear and trembling (Gal. 6:1).

12: Discerning Culture

One cannot very well develop Christian culture if one is receiving and living out a different worldview. If Christians are to retain a Christian world and life view and cultural outworking, they must first honestly examine what they believe and how they live it out. There is no sense in lying to oneself. Therefore, the following material will help the reader discern cultural expressions in order to produce a distinctively Christian culture.

THE ETHICAL ELEMENT

Assessing the moral value of an entire culture is no different from assessing any one human action or expression. While the Bible does not address culture, art, and entertainment directly, it is assumed that these things are subsumed under the rest of life. It is only because much of the Christian West has turned antinomian that Christians are reticent to apply the law of God to the arts. However, when Christians hold the Ten Commandments of God in reverence, I believe they will produce God-glorifying art and participate in God-glorifying entertainment. In the last days, Christians will be known as those who keep the commandments of God according to Revelation 14:12. At the very least, this means that we will give heed to the commandments of God in our day-to-day activities and cultural work. The commandments regulate our lives, framing our actions and our cultural expressions. It is not enough to merely profess appreciation for God and for His commandments. Mere lip service is self-deceiving if there is no concomitant incarnation of that profession.

Therefore, the Christian will self-consciously promote, defend, and obey the commandments of God in his or her artistic expressions... including these objective commands:

Thou shalt have no other gods before me.

Honor thy father and thy mother.

Thou shalt not commit adultery.

When a believer delights in the law of God after the inward man (Rom. 7:22), his delight will betray itself in his cultural creations. Of course, sinless perfection is not possible this side of glory. Nonetheless, a truly Christian culture does set a trajectory towards the keeping of these commandments. Since human society has a corporeal connectedness to it, Christians who lead in art, politics, and business will sanctify or preserve the culture of a nation to some extent. This is how a Christian cultural denominator forms.

THE FAITH ELEMENT - WHICH FAITH OOZES FROM THE CULTURAL EXPRESSION?

As already mentioned in the third chapter, art and culture always reflect the fundamental heart commitments of the artistic creators. A tree is known by its fruit (Matt. 12:33). In a world of a hundred Christs and a thousand counterfeit gods, this principle is a handy way to identify true faith.

Christians believe in the reality of sin and death, but they also believe in the resurrection of the body. This strongly hopeful perspective is so fundamental to the Christian faith and worldview that it cannot but reveal itself in mannerisms, clothing, burial practices, holidays, sabbaths, and music. When a teen raised in a Christian home is infatuated with death, hangs a skull around his neck, and enjoys Death Metal Rock and angry "rape rap," it seems the doctrine of the resurrection hasn't penetrated his heart. Sure, he's parroted the words of the Apostle's Creed on Sunday mornings since he was three years old, but parrots aren't known for their faith. A tree is known by its fruit. It doesn't matter how much the young man insists that he believes the Gospel, or how many "Grace Evangelical" churches he has attended. If he does not believe in the resurrection as indicated by his life, then he does not believe the Gospel of Christ (1 Cor. 15:3-4). He cannot be buried with Christ or risen with Him in newness of life. This is extremely important, especially for those who have fooled themselves into thinking they are Christians when they are only participating in the Western apostasy. While in the midst of such an apostasy, it is a good time for all of us to ask the million dollar question, "Do I really believe in the resurrection of Jesus Christ, and do I identify with it such that I believe that I will be resurrected? How is this manifested day to day in my own life?"

Escapism, decadence, drugs, and Death Metal are not known for the resurrection joy and peace they produce. It is fair to ask the question, "Does the frantic screaming and relentless banging noise communicate the kingdom message of peace and joy?" (Rom. 14:12). Does the average teen ooze the resurrection of Christ? If so, why does he comes across as more glum, distracted, and sullen than ever? Could this have something to do with the music piped through his earbuds and the media he consumes? The whole cultural experience of the postmodern teen is not exactly bathed in resurrection life. Therefore, his clothing, facial expressions, values, and music preferences will not emphasize resurrection.

My wife and I visited two malls in a large city while on vacation: one upscale, and the other middle class. At my first glance it was clear that the difference was in the degree of self-conscious adherence to nihilism. The upscale mall contained even more tattoos, more anorexia, more holes in the scruffy jeans (at $200 a pair), and more grunge than the middle-class mall. In both malls, the Urban Decay makeup line featured the "smog" look, the "trash" look, etc. This is what a society looks like that does not have hope in the resurrection, and young people especially will freely admit that they do not believe in the resurrection of Jesus Christ.

Now if there were Christians who believed in the resurrection of Christ, what would they look like? Would their faith be evident in their cultural expressions? I believe so.

In his treatment of Christian liberty in Romans 14, Paul wraps up the discussion with one powerful statement: "Whatsoever is not of faith is sin" (Rom. 14:23). This is another overarching principle which must be brought to bear in every cultural act or experience. Where a man acts as a result of his faith in God and his faith in the death and resurrection of Christ, he will contribute to Christian culture. Where he acts sinfully, he is not enjoying the benefits of Christ's cleansing blood or the resurrection life of Christ. Where he fears man, where he fears losing the honor of men, where he does not fear God, and where he seeks his own honor, he does not act in faith.

TRUTH AND BEAUTY

In order to pass the biblical test, good cultural expression must be true, honorable, pure, lovely, and of good report, according to the clear description in Philippians 4:8. Thus, a story or a song may present reality in its true light, but only if it is framed in God's world, God's judgment, God's redemption, and God's resurrection. We may sing of pain and death, but we perform against the backdrop of resurrection. Conversely, the pagans sing of parties and fun, but they perform against the backdrop of death and hell. Sometimes death and hell is the theme and content of their songs, not just the backdrop. Their entire perspective exudes hopelessness. On the other hand, the Christian presents the clearest concept of reality and the most pronounced hope for the future. This perspective was well understood by Isaac Watts, who wrote, "Must I be carried to the skies on flowery beds of ease, while others fought to win the prize and sailed through bloody seas? Sure I must fight if I would reign, increase my courage Lord. I'll bear the toil endure the pain supported by thy Word." If the believer is in the business of producing art or entertainment, he must offer a culture of truth and beauty and hope.

THE SUBJECTIVE PERSPECTIVE - WHAT'S THE HEART MOTIVE?

The subjective perspective addresses the internal motive within each person that drives culture and all of human action. While God assigns principles or laws to govern human action, the internal heart motive is equally important. God wants us to love Him with our heart, soul, mind, and strength (Deut. 6:4). He wants us to do things with the intent of glorifying Him (1 Cor. 10:31). Simply put, if our hearts are not inclined towards God in this way, we will not produce good culture.

When we are thinking about culture and art, it is critical that we discern the hearts and lives of those who produce the art. This may be detected in the corpus of their work, their biographies, and their testimonies. Motive is critical to producing that which is good. In order to have God-glorifying culture, a sanctified motive must be present somewhere within the process since human society operates in a corporeal (or covenantal) way. There are elements of Christian (or Christ-incarnated) culture to be found here and there throughout the cultures of the world. Humanists may easily perform Handel's *The Messiah* or Bach's *Jesu, Joy of Man's Desiring* either poorly or admirably. They may misinterpret Bach's music and motive (which, by his own confession was "Soli Deo Gloria"). Even so, it would be hard to purge all of Christ out of Bach, as it would be impossible to purge all of Bach out of Bach. Somewhere in the development of Western culture, there were Christians who wrote their music and sang their Psalms for the love of God and to the glory of God, not for the glory of man. These cultural roots are not easily overcome, even in an apostate world.

WRONG GODS, FLAWED GODS

"These are, indeed, Homer's fictions, but he attributed divine attributes to sinful men, that crimes might not be accounted crimes, and that whoever committed such crimes might appear to imitate the celestial gods and not abandoned men." (Augustine, *Confessions* 1.16)

The heart of the producer and the artist really matters. While it is impossible to judge the heart motive of every person engaging the culture, the cultural systems themselves will reveal their ultimate commitments openly. This is helpful in the analysis.

As previously mentioned, modern culture is primarily formed around a Pop-star "machine," which has mostly developed in the United

States and England (the last of the Western empires). It is hard to imagine what music and motion pictures would look like without Elvis Presley, Madonna, Michael Jackson, The Beatles, Mel Gibson, Humphrey Bogart, Clint Eastwood, Tom Cruise, Will Smith, Kim Basinger, and Marilyn Monroe. In order to better understand this Pop-star system, it is best to compare it to the historical pattern of Rome. According to Augustine, fame and honor are of the highest value in the city of man. In his exhaustive work on humanist culture, Augustine describes the most powerful motive underlying the city of man as "the love of praise."

Augustine states, "It pleased God that there should also arise a Western empire, which, though later in time, should be more illustrious in extent and greatness. He purposely granted it to such men as, for sake of honor, and praise, and glory, consulted well for their country, in whose glory they sought their own, and whose safety they did not hesitate to prefer to their own, suppressing the desire of wealth and many other vices for this one vice, namely, the love of praise. For he has the soundest perception who recognizes that even the love of praise is a vice."[1]

This commentary is important because our present cultural situation is more similar to Rome than to any other time and place in history, and Augustine has much to say concerning that rotting city.

Motivated by the love of praise, empowered by self-faith or self-confidence, aided by demonic powers, the City of Man creates the stars. However, in the City of God, it is fear of God, faith, love, and humility which are preeminent. Generally, the musicians and actors who seek stardom will reject the neighborhood theater and the local coffee house in favor of the big stage. Their larger-than-life personas are developed by handlers behind the screen, and the movie stars become gods. Of course they are flawed gods, but all sins and indiscretions are forgiven them by their admirers, for the same reason that the Greeks insisted on flawed gods: "That whoever committed such crimes might appear to imitate the celestial gods." Nobody wants a righteous god when they have rejected righteousness themselves.

Thus, it should come as no surprise the Pop-star system first created the fictional character Hannah Montana, using Miley Cyrus at fourteen years of age. The Hollywood machine took the young Pop star into soft porn spreads at age sixteen, then on to her drug-infested orgies at age twenty. The paparazzi, gossip magazines, record companies, the promoters and handlers, the media, and the talent operate as an unholy team to create the gods of our culture. The drugs, divorces, orgies, and police arrests all play a part in defining these modern-day gods. This is what the reprobate world wants. Most of the celebrities must commit to some level of Christian apostasy. Occasionally, someone like Tim Tebow (the Christian football player who won the Heisman trophy in 2007), or Kirk Cameron (a Christian actor) will break the mold, but the god-makers don't tolerate a man very long who worships the true God in the end zone. Obviously, the gods who take their position at the top of the pantheon cannot be Christians. The first baseball star, Babe Ruth, was known for his infidelities and divorces, and this was only the beginning of a long line of scandals that marked the gods of the twentieth and twenty-first centuries. Of course this whole system flies in the face of the first commandment: "Thou shalt have no other gods before me" (Ex. 20:3). Christians should be particularly annoyed when culture's stars receive more adulation at concerts and in newspapers than the true and living God (who is rarely recognized except when His name is blasphemed).

The Hollywood-Nashville star system is almost entirely reliant on ego and self-confidence. The love of praise, says Augustine, "is so hostile to a pious faith, if the love of glory be greater in the heart than the fear or love of God."[2] Therefore, Christians will be driven more by faith in God and love for God. Thus motivated, there is no reason why they should not produce excellent work, and apply greater diligence to their arts and crafts. However, if they should fall to the lure of fame and fortune, they will be cursed with double-mindedness in their work. Occasionally, artists will break the mold and return to the coffee houses and local theaters. By the end of his career, Johnny Cash preferred singing "I've Been Working on the Railroad" and "Far Side Banks of Jordan" over "Cocaine Blues." No longer gods, they return to being real people back to singing real songs. Interestingly, this process is described in Cash's song, "Ballad of a Teenage Queen."

When it comes to recorded music, it is almost impossible to completely separate the message and the performance from the life of the performer. As the story goes, the legendary Hank Williams was sitting in a limo, singing "I Saw the Light" with Minnie Pearl. Then, he turned to her and said, "There ain't no light, Minnie, there ain't no light."[3] How can we believe a man who does not believe in the light while he sings about the light? How can we take him seriously? If a man is "getting laid and saved" in the same Country album, is he really getting saved? During a period of great apostasy like this one, discerning Christians are pressed to sift through the thousands of counterfeits to find the real deal. Elvis Presley was not very believable in his recording of "(There'll Be) Peace in the Valley (for Me)" at 22 years of age while he was simultaneously working the charts with "Jail House Rock" and "Hound Dog." There wasn't much peace in the valley for a man who died of a drug overdose at forty-two years of age. We are more convinced by the hoarse renderings of this song by Johnny Cash in his sixty-seventh year. It was also hard to believe that Elvis believed in God, when Elvis was treated like a god by a crowd of screaming girls (who can still be heard in his live recording of "Peace in the Valley").

Granted, it is hard to critique the Christian who professes to love God and to seek God's glory, while in actuality he doesn't love God and he seeks his own glory. We critique the subjective and we would be accused of ad hominem. Nonethless, the art produced for the glory of man will detract from Christian culture, and draw other unsuspecting Christians into its web. Though God is sovereign over these matters, we do well to be mindful of the eventualities of cheating God of his glory. Pastors and Christian leaders must engage in regular cultural analysis and commentary if they want to salvage the faith in the next generation.

The motive to excellence is most often lodged in the drive towards fame and fortune, in that the highest value in the city of man is the praise of man. Nonetheless, Christians must hold tightly to a different motive. As the creation of God, we work to the glory of God. As the servants and friends of the Lord Jesus Christ, we serve with all the love and joy than ever a man served. As the recipients of talents from the King in the greatest Kingdom in the world, we address ourselves to multiply these talents with a thousand times more motivation than those in the City of Man. If pride and human accolades provide the highest motive in that city, we have to believe that the accomplishments will at some point fall short of excellence. Pride always comes before a fall (Prov. 16:18). But if a man hones his talents according to the higher motives, he will produce something of outstanding excellence, and nothing can inhibit his achievement but his own pride. Thus, the highest form of music will always come from a man who places the acronym "S.D.G." on every piece that he creates.[4]

EDIFICATION - WHAT DOES THE CULTURAL EXPERIENCE PRODUCE?

Perhaps the best test for any cultural form or experience is seen in the end results. Is the art form actually producing something good? For a Christian artist, it takes a discerning heart, and often a meaningful relationship with one's audience to know whether or not the art he is producing is edifying. The artist who stands at the greatest distance from his audience has the least awareness of the effect of his art. This should be of concern to many a Christian Pop star.

Shortly before he died, Larry Norman, the father of Christian Contemporary music, suggested on his blog that the Christian church should abandon all music for some years, and just "teach the Word." He was concerned that the church and the musical expression of the church that he was familiar with had become weak and immature. Was he condemning the form that he had promoted for the majority of his adult life?

When our children were young, we allowed them to watch Disney movies. One day, my five-year-old son was chasing his sister around the house, hollering, "I'm going to kill you!" We came to find out he had picked up the line from one of the movies he had seen (*Jungle Book*), and we promptly yanked the selection from the shelf. Parents must monitor the edification factor of the books read, the movies watched, and the musical entertainment ingested by the members of his household.

For example, parents should be aware of the books their children are reading and the effects on attitudes, perspectives, and behavior. Some books contribute to depression and even suicide. Too much escapist fiction often produces dissatisfaction and discontentment with true reality (sometimes perceived as "boring"). Many teenage adventure stories glorify and idealize a life of fame and fortune, a life without sin and consequence, and a life without service to God. This may very well attract children into its godless lifestyle. If children have vicariously experienced this life through the characters in the story, the problem may be even worse. After all, their "real world" is nothing but strict parents, long boring church services, spankings for disobedience, chores, and "meaningless" homework. If what they read in their free time yields discontentment and rebellion, parents would do well to reconsider these genres, or at least the sheer quantity of the books in these genres that their children are consuming.

In fact, many parents are rethinking the entire worldview that produced so much disposable time for entertainment. Many families are reviving the family-based economy.[5] For 5900 years, the family economy was the means by which families trained their children to work, transition into adulthood, and carry on civilization. It has only been in the last several generations that rich nations have corrupted their youth through excessive entertainment, peer culture, and sexual "freedom." The breakdown of faith and with it, culture, happens when fathers stop making the call—when they leave it up to Lady Gaga and her producers to design the cultural fare for their kids.

It does take special discernment to know which media sources are producing which character issues in a family. However, I am hopeful that most families have already figured out that rewarding a ten-year-old son with six hours of games and media after he has finished four hours of boring schoolwork each day is a recipe for disaster. There is hardly a better way to destroy the character and economic viability of the next generation. Without restoring robust family economies in which young boys and girls can use their time wisely, Western society will continue to see national character languish.

DEFINING EDIFICATION

"Let every one of us please his neighbor for his good to edification." (Rom. 15:2)

"Let no corrupt communication proceed out of your mouth, but that which is good to the use of edifying, that it may minister grace unto the hearers." (Eph. 4:29)

Edification involves the improvement of a person, but one can only define improvement in the context of a certain worldview. What constitutes edification for a materialist Marxist is very different for the Christian who will be concerned with spiritual growth. At the end of the day, we want to see more spiritual growth, first of all, in addition to emotional encouragement and intellectual development.

The effects of certain cultural experiences also may be analyzed both individually and in connection with other experiences. What may be acceptable in small doses may not be acceptable in large doses. What may be edifying for a smaller audience may not be equally edifying for a larger audience. Artists and producers are somewhat responsible for how their work is received on the macro scale. While they may not have control over how every individual receives the work, they should concern themselves with how the majority will receive it.

DISCERNING EDIFICATION

Our family has not had access to cable television in our home for at least five years. Recently, to get a flavor for the present offerings, I spent about ten minutes flipping through the channels in a hotel room. MTV featured an amateur video of a bride throwing up on herself at her wedding, played in slow motion repeatedly. Another channel featured a violent torture scene that I could not watch straight through, but as I flipped past the channel several times,

I noted that the gore was beyond anything I'd ever witnessed on television in previous decades. Another channel featured one of many scores of true crime dramatizations, in which I learned about a really kind homosexual man who took good care of his butterfly collection and in his free time welcomed in stray homosexuals from off the street, for who knows what reasons. Not surprisingly, he was murdered by one of his new "friends." The advertisements reverted between pharmaceuticals introducing new psychotropic drugs and attorneys looking to sue over the last batch of psychotropic drugs that had produced enlarged breasts on little boys. It is a strange world out there, but you may not realize this if you have already plugged yourself into the matrix. On another channel, a sitcom relied entirely on sexual innuendo and references to body parts for illicit laughs. Cursing, the abuse of God's name, and references to defecation flowed almost without respite. I turned off the trash, wondering what effect such a constant barrage of the unpleasant, the coarse, the impure, the unedifying, and the all that lacks virtue might produce upon the viewing audience that absorbs it day in and day out. More than ever before, post-modern nihilists delight in that which is profane and not beautiful—such as a bride throwing up on herself. Remarkably, this is the highest entertainment value for billion dollar networks in a society in its death throes.

Lest any think that my purpose is to curtail Christian liberty, I am not saying that it is a sin to watch television. That would be far too simple a conclusion for this discussion on culture. Nonetheless, it is a sin for a father to allow his family to spend two hours watching television or a movie while failing to assess whether or not it is edifying for his family. To not make this call is a sin of omission, and this sin is committed daily in "Christian" families around the country. If a father should decide that it is a beautiful and edifying thing for his family to watch a bride throwing up on herself for hours on end, I would have to question his discernment and wisdom. I would challenge him to love God with more of his mind and heart, and then tell him to watch his children more carefully to determine whether they are loving God more over the months and years.

EXCESS AND IDOLATRY

Excesses and the idolatry associated with them are especially evident when other priorities are displaced. Idolatry in the heart displaces the importance of God and His worship. The Super Bowl can be idolized enough to take priority over God's worship and the fellowship of the saints on Sunday. In today's culture, depersonalized media and money can easily trump family relationships and true friendship.

If a cultural experience is producing addictions or fetishisms, it becomes idolatrous. But these idols can be crushed by faith in the risen Christ, confession, self-denial, fasting, and worship of the true God. According to CovenantEyes.com, 80% of young men (18-25 years of age)[6] are addicted to pornography, meaning they visit online pornography sites weekly or monthly. Viewing pornography is a violation of both the 1st and the 7th commandments. The motive is self-love and the effects of it are defrauding and depersonalizing. Paul encourages the Ephesian believers to "redeem the time, for the days are evil (*porneia*)" (Eph. 5:16). It is a huge risk for young men to spend hours upon hours surfing the internet and engaging in mindless, useless distractions. Should any soldier in combat be watching birds or picking daisies while hand grenades are exploding around him, he would be deemed insane. This is not the time for netting butterflies. This is war. If anything, it is the thousands of distractions that are killing our youth, undermining the character of nations, and breaking down the faith.

THE GOOD LIFE

The good life is a combination of work and rest because that is the way it was designed by God. If God is good and gives us what is good, then we accept His definition of the good life. While the world is "entertaining themselves to death," we are working and resting. This is the essence of the fourth commandment. We work for God and we rest in God (Heb. 4:10).

God designed certain aesthetic experiences that delight the human soul, which include sexuality, wine, food, and music. Although some Christian ascetics have denied themselves pleasure so as to avoid idolatry, there is nothing in Scripture that advocates this practice. To insist that there is nothing pleasurable or should be nothing pleasurable about sexuality, wine, food, or music would only deny reality, God's created order of all things.

Deuteronomy 12 and 14 present the biblical principles relating to the use of food and wine for celebration. The proper enjoyment of God's gifts happens when they are received *coram deo* (before the face of God).

> *"And ye shall rejoice before the Lord your God, ye, and your sons, and your daughters, and your menservants, and your maidservants, and the Levite that is within your gates; forasmuch as he hath no part nor inheritance with you."* (Deut. 12:12)

We rejoice before God, and in community with others. A father takes his ten-year-old son to a fair and buys him a ticket for the Ferris wheel. As the boy enjoys the ride, he waves at his father and hollers to his father down below, "Thanks Dad! I'm having a good time!" What father doesn't enjoy watching his son enjoying himself? What father doesn't enjoy giving his child good gifts? God requires our gratitude. He wants us rejoicing in His presence. We are not to be men hiding out in our basements, giving undue regard to online pornography and shameful, sinful acts while running from God and not rejoicing in His presence.

One of the reasons why Christians have a hard time worshiping on Sunday mornings is because they have not worshiped on Saturday nights. A professing Christian may spend a few hours in a movie theater watching a motion picture that fails to give God glory. He doesn't worship God in the theater at the end of the movie. Then he enjoys intimacy with his wife at home but he doesn't worship God for His benefits. This man is very distant from God during the week, and then he finds himself in a worship service on a Sunday morning having a hard time turning on the "worship switch."

REPENTANCE

Modern entertainment for many of us has become "the devil's

substitute for joy," as Leonard Ravenhill would say. How many of us have given way to this idolatry, seeking comfort and respite from the stresses and agonies of life? But alas, these idols "comfort in vain" (Zech. 10:2). It is usually by fasts (including media fasts) that we discover the idolatries of the heart. For a period of time, we go through withdrawals. Here we begin to see the damage done by the visual medium or some other form of entertainment: the self-centeredness, the depersonalized relationships, and the grieving of the Spirit. As repentance proceeds, the psyche endures the misery stage. On one hand, we have lost the pseudo-joy provided by the idol. But we also suffer the chastisement of God until He restores to us the joy of our salvation (Ps. 51:12). Gradually over months and years, the Word of God and the promises of God begin to shine again. The story of Christ becomes real. Hope in the promises begins to produce a little glimmer of joy here, and a little glimmer of joy there. Quantity becomes quality. Quantity Word time becomes quality Word time. Whereas we may have spent three hours in a day seeking pseudo-joy in entertainment, now we mine true joy in Word and prayer four to five hours a day. There is careful meditation on the Word; a scanning and rescanning for a promise that will comfort and a story that will buttress faith. This is the process of repentance, and this author speaks of it from personal experience.

DISCERNING THE TRENDS

It is helpful to know that Doris Day wasn't riding on wrecking balls in the nude in 1954, and Nat King Cole wasn't referring to his mother as a female dog in 1958. A recent survey considered the number of sexual innuendoes and sexual scenes in one television season selected from each decade, from the 1950s to the 2000s. It should be no surprise that the survey reported an increase by orders of magnitude every decade or so. However, the same cannot be said for popular culture in England or America in the latter part of the 18th century.

Every Christian man needs to understand the trends of the times. Every society at every stage in history represents different trajectories. What effect might this knowledge have upon Christian families? I would think that there would be fewer families embracing the brave new world that is hell-bent on suicide.

More than any other genre, Country music represents the cultural heartbeat of the heartland in this country. If you want to follow the trajectory of Christian apostasy, you can do no better than to watch the Country charts. I worked as a radio personality on a station that carried a country music format in the 1980s. I tried to avoid playing the adultery and drunkenness songs in the assigned rotations, but this rather limited the selections. At its best, Country music provides respect for a heritage, faith and family. However at its worse, the genre corrupts those standards generation by generation. In the 1950s, it was appropriate to speak of cheating in a pejorative sense as in Hank Williams' "Your Cheatin' Heart." Every culture in decline will experience its mini-revolutions against the past. The revolution in the heartland came in 1961 with Leroy Van Dyke's "Walk on By"[7] a bona fide cheating song clearly promoting an illicit adulterous relationship. It was a culture defining song for the American heartland, as the hit remained at the top of the charts for nineteen weeks, *a record that stood for fifty-one years.* Bobby Bare's protagonist caved to adultery in "Margie's at the Lincoln Park Inn" (1969). There is a touch of shame, but not enough to bring about repentance in this hit song. Following the sexual revolution of the 1960s, Country music joins the crowd with open promotions of fornication, as in Kris Kristofferson's "Help Me Make It through the Night." By the 1980s and 1990s, it would hardly be an exaggeration to say that most "love" songs in the Country music format assumed fornicating relationships. The popular music genres only reflect the heart of an apostate nation determined to abandon all standards of morality. The Country music genre finally capitulated to ultimate moral decay in 2014, when Kacey Musgraves won Album of the Year at the Academy of Country Music Awards, the Country Music Association Awards, and the Grammys for her album *Same Trailer, Different Park.*[8] Her lead single, "Follow Your Arrow" explicitly endorsed total sexual autonomy, homosexuality, and recreational drug use. In the same song, she mocked the Christian church for its hypocrisy and suggested autonomy or a total rejection of biblical morality as the solution. That was the same year a major motion picture called *Dallas Buyer's Club* took home several Oscars. The film portrayed a cowboy given over to complete heterosexual license who contracts the AIDS disease. Both the cowboy and his audience discover that an anti-homosexual bias is untenable, judgmental and hypocritical in the AIDS ward of a hospital. Lesson learned: if we accept abominable activity A, then of course we must also accept abominable activity B. This is the logic of moral apostasy. When the corruption makes it into the heartland, there isn't much left to salvage.

Nathaniel Hawthorne's famous final words in *The Scarlet Letter* apply here. "Be True. Be True. Be True." Above all, the humanist must be true to herself. Kacey Musgraves and Hester Prynne must reject all hypocrisy along with the law of God. "Be what you really want to be. Negate the old Christian order. Forget pretending to emulate the old Christian order. If you prefer some sexual perversion, just admit it. Come out of the closet if you prefer the homosexual lifestyle. Be true. Be true to yourself."

This is the trajectory on which the arrow of popular media and Top 40 Country radio stations move. This is how the heartland apostatizes. Undiscerning, unrestrained participation in these cultural systems will result in softening of moral standards everywhere, and the popular acceptance of a "progressive" agenda. Given these cultural trajectories, Christian families must think carefully before setting their car radios and internet connections to Top 40 Country and Pop formats. When their teenage kids prefer the cool Top 40 and Hot Country radio stations to a more discerning standard, the generational apostasy metastasizes.

To better understand the flow of culture in historical context, suppose that Augustine was transported into a twenty-first century theater for a screening of *The Hunger Games*. This outside perspective of recent cultural developments would be eye opening, to say the least. In his film review, Augustine discovers something in the film strangely reminiscent of what he had witnessed in the Roman games as a youth, except that these new games would come across as a little insipid to him: they would seem pitiful attempts to replicate the paganism of a bygone era—human beings degrading themselves, yes, but nothing like what the Romans did. Then, he would catch a whiff of Christ fragrance, a Christ memory, even in this godless story. "Christ has been here," he would say. He would see the self-sacrifice, and the unmistakable hesitation to participate in the murderous games, the horror of it. He would hear the taking of the Lord's name in vain—all of this unfamiliar to the pagan Roman culture. Nonetheless, he would also sense that Christ had departed, or rather, that the author, the actors, the antagonists, and the protagonists had all departed from Christ. Augustine would certainly note the apostasy. Yet, I think he would leave the theater with a satisfied sense of Christ's victory in history. No matter how badly the apostates desire to restore the old pagan Roman world (as Adolf Hitler and others have tried to do), they cannot possibly reverse 2000 years of the reign of Jesus Christ over history.

CULTURAL ISLANDS

I hope the reader can see by now that there is something very wrong with an apostate culture that celebrates homosexual weddings and Satanic rites at the 2014 Grammy Awards. Christians in the third century were beginning to transform pagan culture into Christian culture. Those of us from the twenty-first century West find ourselves in a different state of affairs. We are watching apostates transform Christian culture into pagan culture or rather into a virulent apostate culture (as church attendance falls from 60% to 6% in England). Thus, when we watch Christians borrow from the Pop culture, we cannot help but think this will produce yet another wave of apostasy rather than transforming pagan culture into Christian culture. Many claim to be sanctifying culture, but in an age of apostasy one must be very suspect of the agenda.

The Babylon that feasts on pleasures, pride, the praise of men, and the lust of the flesh always passes away (Isa. 47, 1 John 2:17). From the historical perspective, no city saturated in debauchery survived. Sodom was the prototype. How can we forget the story of the sudden destruction of Pompeii? Here was a city known as the New Orleans or San Francisco of the ancient world with its debauched artistic forms and unrestrained sexual license. Institutionalized cultural forms of idolatry whether they are pleasure, fame, or the praise of men will always come to an end quickly and without warning (Gen. 19:13-16, Is. 47:11, Rev. 18:8, Pompeii). This was the fate of the Roman empire, and why would God not hold the apostate Christian countries to the same account?

Therefore, Christians are called to come out of Babylon (Rev. 18:4), to escape Sodom with Lot and never turn back (Luke 17:32). The world they escape is clearly defined in 1 John 2:16 as the world made of lust and pride—that which will not commit to following the will of God (1 John 2:17). This is the most condensed definition of worldly culture to be found in Scripture, and true Christians cannot but abandon the dying culture that passes away. They will carefully and assiduously weed worldliness out of their cultural work. Should any fail to identify the lust of the eyes and the pride of life in the 2014 Grammys, or should they fail to detect rebellion against God's will in Lady Gaga's "Born This Way," they must have already joined the apostasy. It may have been slightly harder to detect the lust of the flesh in Leroy Van Dyke's "Walk On By." The less discerning would have missed the lust of the eyes and the lust of the flesh in the Hollywood blockbuster, *Some Like it Hot* (1959). How many Christians failed to recognize the lust of the flesh in Debbie Boone's "You Light Up My Life" in the 1970s?[9] "How can it be wrong if it feels so right?" What was this Christian woman thinking when she sang those words a hundred times over in concerts throughout the 70s and 80s? Was she doing the will of the Father, or passing away with Joe Brooks, the world, and "the lusts thereof?" (1 John 2:17).

Apostasy comes easier and faster now than it did in the 1800s. Church attendance is falling off faster than ever. Christian Contemporary Music stars are admitting to homosexual lifestyles, and increasingly accepted by their colleagues.[10] There is no place for naiveté at this point. Christian involvement in popular culture can be counter-productive, because Christian musicians, media reps, and actors are often the most immature and least equipped to enter the cultural wars. They are drawn to the glitz and the glamour of it, or the praise of men. Then, they are consumed by it. Actually, it should be the other way around. The meek will inherit the earth (Matt. 5:5). The reason that Christians do not inherit the earth, is because they are not meek as yet. Until Christians become meek, they cannot inherit the earth and thereby inherit the culture. It is the spiritually mature whose obedience is fulfilled that will "cast down imaginations" and engage in the cultural wars (2 Cor. 10:4-6).

There is no room for rosy eyed acceptance of the cultural decay around us. Highly suspect will be any Christian literary and cultural critic who makes too much room for Lady Gaga, Harry Potter, Hester Prynne, Huckleberry Finn, James Bond, Katniss Everdeen, Joe Brooks, Leroy Van Dyke, and *Star Trek: Into Darkness*. Those who enthusiastically embrace these cultural icons appear to be happy with the macro-cultural trends of the Christian apostate world. That being the case, what does this say about their faith, their worldview, and their own cultural trajectories? Could it be that they have embraced the tattooed Jesus—the false Christs of culture? Indeed, many have been wooed by a false prophet, a false priest, a false redeemer, and a false king. They have been rescued from the wrong sins and have taken on the wrong view of reality, truth, and ethics. They have embraced the wrong religion, and they have joined the apostasy.

The true Christ saves us from our sin—both the guilt and the corruption of it. He demands a transformation of culture and life according to the will of God (Rom. 12:1-2) and according to the commandments of God (Rev. 12:17, 14:12). So Christians will by definition produce transformed music, film, and culture. However, for now Christians will be pressed into more distinctive cultural islands, while the macro peels off into decadence and nihilism. Nathan Clark George, Steve Camp, and Michael Card are persona non grata in the CCM market. Film producers such as Stephen Kendrick and Rich Christiano must work outside Hollywood and create their own markets. Reports say Christian singer, Natalie Grant walked out of the 2014 Grammys in disgust with the Satanic orgies and homosexual weddings.[11] Perhaps she should have left twenty years ago.

"And what concord hath Christ with Belial? or what part hath he that believeth with an infidel? And what agreement hath the temple

of God with idols? For ye are the temple of the living God; as God hath said, I will dwell in them, and walk in them; and I will be their God, and they shall be my people. Wherefore come out from among them, and be ye separate, saith the Lord, and touch not the unclean thing; and I will receive you." (2 Cor. 6:15-17)

Notes

Preface

1. "After Election 2012: Living in the New Moral Landscape," http://www.christianitytoday.com/ct/2012/november-web-only/election-2012-reaction-christian-response-new-moral-landsca.html

2. "Religion Among the Millennials," http://www.pewforum.org/2010/02/17/religion-among-the-millennials/

3. "It's Not Just Frozen: Most Disney Movies are Pro Gay," http://www.theatlantic.com/entertainment/archive/2014/04/its-not-just-frozen-disney-has-always-been-subtly-pro-gay/361060/?google_editors_picks=true

Introduction

1. "Lady Gaga and the Death of Sex," http://www.thesundaytimes.co.uk/sto/public/magazine/article389697.ece

2. "Warhol's $100 Soup Earned Dealer $15 Million, Returns to L.A.," http://www.bloomberg.com/news/2011-08-11/warhol-s-100-soup-earned-canny-dealer-15-million-returns-to-los-angeles.html

3. T.S. Eliot, *Christianity and Culture: The Idea of a Christian Society and Notes Towards the Definition of Culture* (Orlando: Mariner Books, 1948).

4. Kevin Swanson, *Apostate: The Men who Destroyed the Christian West* (Parker: Generations with Vision, 2013).

1: Following the Trajectory

1. "Fertility in China," http://countryeconomy.com/demography/fertility/chinasts

"Fertility in South Korea," http://countryeconomy.com/demography/fertility/south-korea

2. It is also possible that the Western missionaries carried something of the existentialism that imploded birth rates in Korea and elsewhere.

3. "Most Americans have had premarital sex, study finds,"http://usatoday30.usatoday.com/news/health/2006-12-19-premarital-sex_x.htm

4. "Porn Stats," http://www.covenanteyes.com/pornstats/

5. "Henry Clay Work," http://en.wikipedia.org/wiki/Henry_Clay_Work

6. "Larry Norman's Tragic Post-Mortem," http://www.worldmag.com/2008/07/larry_norman_s_tragic_post_mortem

7. "Study Shows Churches Make Contemporary Shift," http://www.christiantoday.com/article/study.shows.churches.make.contemporary.shift/226.htm.

8. "God-Fearing Angus T. Jones Tells People to Stop Watching Two and a Half Men," http://www.starpulse.com/news/index.php/2012/11/27/godfearing_angus_t_jones_tells_people_

9. "Carrie Underwood Reaffirms Gay Marriage Support in Allure Interview," http://www.huffingtonpost.com/2013/01/16/carrie-underwood-gay-marriage-country-singer_n_2488967.html

10. "Katy Perry 'Dark Horse' Meaning: Grammy's 'Satanic' Performance About Drugs," http://

global.christianpost.com/news/katy-perry-dark-horse-meaning-grammys-satanic-performance-about-drugs-video-113600/

11. Some will suggest that Christians should dispense altogether with all holidays bearing any pagan heritage whatsoever. This is both simplistic and unrealistic, given that there are many pagan roots in human culture, some of which do not bear ungodly or immoral associations. There is also Christian liberty in relation to celebrating days and seasons (Rom. 14). Moreover, we are looking for a direction, not perfection, in our Christian life and culture, whether in the individual or corporate sense. Suffice it to say that the modern celebration of Halloween is a bad trajectory for those who wish to commemorate that which is good and godly.

12. Margaret Paton, *Letters from the South Seas* (Edinburgh: Banner of Truth, 2003).

13. *Da Jesus Book: Hawaiian Pidgin New Testament* (Orlando: Wycliffe Bible Translators, 2000), Matthew 13:1-4.

2: Culture Changers

1. "Carrie Underwood Reaffirms Gay Marriage Support in Allure Interview," http://www.huffingtonpost.com/2013/01/16/carrie-underwood-gay-marriage-country-singer_n_2488967.html

2. Augustine, "City of God," *The Nicene & Post Nicene Fathers: First Series*, ed. Phillip Schaff, trans. Marcus Dods (Peabody: Hendrickson, 2004), 2:97.

3. Ibid., 2:205.

4. see www.transparencyinternational.com

3: Hip-Hop

1. "Lecrae," http://en.wikipedia.org/wiki/Lecrae

2. "Lecrae speak of Hip-Hop Relevance," http://www.bpnews.net/bpnews.asp?ID=40684.

3. Jeff Chang, "It's a Hip-Hop World," Foreign Policy, November/December 2007, 58-65.

4. "Hip-Hop," http://en.wikipedia.org/wiki/Hip_hop

4: Christian Kitsch

1. Lori Preuitt, "Alchohol, Drugs Killed Thomas Kinkade: Autopsy," http://www.nbcbayarea.com/news/local/Alcohol-Drugs-Killed-Thomas-Kinkade-Autopsy-150518425.html

2. "Autopsy: Thomas Kinkade Died of Alcohol, Valium Overdose," http://articles.orlandosentinel.com/2012-05-07/news/ktla-thomas-kinkade-dead_1_thomas-kinkade-light-talents

3. Franky Schaeffer, *Addicted to Mediocrity: Contemporary Christians and the Arts* (Wheaton: Crossway, 1981).

4. "Composer Joseph Brooks 'suicide a tragedy for everybody,' says His Defense Lawyer," http://www.nydailynews.com/news/crime/composer-joseph-brooks-suicide-tragedy-defense-lawyer-article-1.142591

5. "Utah No. 1 in online porn subscriptions, report says," http://www.deseretnews.com/article/705288350/Utah-No-1-in-online-porn-subscriptions-report-says.html?pg= "Church Attendance Lowest in New England, Highest in South," http://www.gallup.com/poll/22579/church-attendance-lowest-new-england-highest-south.aspx

6. John Calvin, *Commentary on the Book of Psalms*, trans. James Anderson (Grand Rapids: Baker, 2003), 1:xxxvii.

7. "The Aesthetics of the Popular Arts," *Journal of Aesthetics and Art Criticism* (Spring 1966), 359.

6: The Tattooed Jesus

1. Eusebius, *Ecclesiastical History*, trans. C.F. Cruse (Peabody: Hendrickson, 2011), 150.

2. Ibid., 151.

3. "Tattoos a 'generational badge' for young adults," http://www.nwitimes.com/news/opinion/forum/tattoos-a-generational-badge-for-young-adults/article_20fb467c-3ed5-56e4-9722-47fbb6a8ea09.html

4. "One in Five U.S. Adults Now Have a Tatoo," http://www.harrisinteractive.com/NewsRoom/HarrisPolls/tabid/447/mid/1508/articleId/970/ctl/ReadCustom%20Default/Default.aspx

5. James Bradley, *Flyboys: A True Story of Courage* (Boston: Little, Brown, and Company, 2003), 246-247.

7: The Cultural Command

1. see Eminem, *The Marshall Mathers LP*. Interscope Records B00004T9UH, compact disc. Originally released in 2000. The LP sold in excess of 20 million copies in 2000. Eminem later apologized to his mother for his abusive language. "Eminem apologizes to his mom in music video 'Headlights' released on Mother's Day, http://www.nydailynews.com/entertainment/music-arts/eminem-apolo-gizes-mom-music-video-headlights-article-1.1788988

2. Jon Savage, *Teenage: The Creation of Youth Culture* (New York: Viking, 2007).

3. Marcel Danesi, *Cool: The Signs and Meanings of Adolescence* (Toronto: University of Toronto Press, 1994).

4. Ibid.

5. Dick Pountain and David Robbins, *Cool Rules: Anatomy of an Attitude* (London: Reaktion Books, 2000).

6. 1 Corinthians 11:4, Every man praying or prophesying, having his head covered, dishonoureth his head.

7. Kenneth A. Myers, *All God's Children and Blue Suede Shoes: Christians and Popular Culture* (Wheaton: Crossway, 1989), 129.

8. Ibid., 100.

9. David Bourdon, *Warhol* (Harry N. Abrams Inc. Publishing, 1995), 110.

10. "Kenny Chesney 'Just Who I Am: Poets & Pirates,'" http://www.gactv.com/gac/ar_az_kenny_chesney/article/0,,gac_26106_5691606,00.html

11. Jean-Paul Sartre, *Nausea*, trans. Lloyd Alexander (New York: New Directions Publishing, 1964), 14-15.

12. Henry Van Til, *The Calvinistic Concept of Culture* (Philadelphia: P&R Publishing, 1959), 57.

8: Wise Discernment for Music in Home and Church

1. "Religion Among the Millennials," http://www.pewforum.org/2010/02/17/religion-among-the-millennials/

2. Lyrics obtained from www.azlyrics.com

9: Entertainment and Metaphor

1. R.J. Rushdoony, *Revolt Against Maturity* (Vallecito: Ross House, 1987), 27.

2. *The Essays of Montaigne*, trans. E.J. Trechmann (New York: Oxford University Press, 1935), 2:291.

3. "Barna Survey Examines Changes in Worldview Among Christians over the Past 13 Years," https://www.barna.org/barna-update/article/21-transformation/252-barna-survey-examines-changes-in-worldview-among-christians-over-the-past-13-years

4. "GTA 5 Sales Hit $1 Billion, Will Outsell Entire Global Music Industry," http://www.fool.com/investing/general/2013/09/28/gta-5-sales-hit-1-billion.aspx

5. "Gartner Says Worldwide Video Game Market to Total $93 Billion in 2013," www.gartner.com/newsroom/id/2614915

6. "Digital Media Beats," http://mashable.com/2013/08/02/digital-media-beats-tv/2. The study was conducted by eMarketer.

7. J.R.R. Tolkien, "On Fairy Stories," http://brainstorm-services.com/wcu-2004/fairystories-tolkien.pdf

8. Ibid.

9. Ibid.

10. "Record First-Day Sales for Last 'Harry Potter' Book," http://www.nytimes.com/2007/07/22/books/22cnd-potter.html?_r=0.

11. "Star Trek: Into Darkness," http://www.movieguide.org/reviews/star-trek-into-darkness.html

12. "Phoenix," http://harrypotter.wikia.com/wiki/Phoenix

13. "Rowling Lets Dumbledore Out of the Closet," http://abcnews.go.com/Entertainment/story?id=3755544

14. "Hogwarts safe for LGBT students? Absolutely, says J.K. Rowling", http://onenewsnow.com/media/2014/12/29/hogwarts-safe-for-lgbt-students-absolutely-says-jk-rowling#.VKQfmyvF-V0

15. Jerram Barrs, *Echoes of Eden: Reflections on Christianity, Literature, and the Arts* (Wheaton: Crossway, 2013), 193-194.

10: Worldviews at the Movies

1. "The Religious Affiliation of the 25 Most Influential Film Directors of All Time," Grewww.adherents.com/movies/adh_dir.html

2. Star Wars: Episode IV – A New Hope, directed by George Lucas (1977; 20th Century Fox), Star Wars: Episode VI – Return of the Jedi, directed by George Lucas (1983: 20th Century Fox).

3. "Humanist Manifesto I," http://americanhumanist.org/Humanism/Humanist_Manifesto_I

4. "Man of Steel (2013)," http://www.imdb.com/title/tt0770828/quotes

5. Ibid.

6. "Man of Steel Promoted to Christian Groups: Warner Bros. Takes Superhero Flick to the Pulpit," http://www.huffingtonpost.com/2013/06/19/man-of-steel-christian-groups_n_3466754.html

7. "The Grey (2011)," http://www.imdb.com/title/tt1601913/quotes?ref_=tt_ql_3

8. "The Lion King (1994)," http://www.imdb.com/title/tt0110357/quotes

9. "Many Americans Mix Multiple Faiths," http://www.pewforum.org/2009/12/09/many-americans-mix-multiple-faiths/

11: The Ethical Level

1. "SufFolk weighs ban on cross-gender clothing for students," http://hamptonroads.com/2012/02/sufFolk-weighs-ban-crossgender-clothing-students

2. "Incest is holy in God's sight?: a Westminster West Grad gets consistent with his R2K," http://americanvision.org/9836/incest-holy-gods-sight-westminster-west-grad-gets-consistent-r2k/

3. "Titanic (1997)," http://www.imdb.com/title/tt0120338/quotes

4. Robert C. Solomon, *Existentialism* (New York: McGraw-Hill, 1974), 1-2.

5. Brian Godawa, *Hollywood Worldviews: Watching Films with Wisdom and Discernment* (Downers Grove: IVP, 2002).

6. "At this point, he is more intense, more insane and much angrier," http://www.indielondon.co.uk/film/red_dragon_feat.html

7. "Obscene" literally means "off stage."

8. "Dang Me," http://en.wikipedia.org/wiki/Dang_Me

9. "Roger Miller," http://en.wikipedia.org/wiki/Roger_Miller, "Dang Me," http://www.allmusic.com/song/dang-me-mt0012521745

10. "Jack Bauer's six degrees of torture: sickest episode of '24' yet," http://www.examiner.com/article/jack-bauer-s-six-degrees-of-torture-sickest-episode-of-24-yet

11. "For millennials, Out-of-Wedlock Childbirth is the Norm," http://www.slate.com/articles/business/moneybox/2014/06/for_millennials_out_of_wedlock_childbirth_is_the_norm_now_what.html

12. "To Hold Senate, Democrats Rely on Single Women," http://www.nytimes.com/2014/07/03/us/single-women-midterm-elections.html?_r=0

13. With box office receipts totaling at $1.2 billion, Frozen stands as the 5th most popular movie of all time.

14. "7 Moments That Made 'Frozen' the Most Progress Disney Movie Ever," http://mic.com/articles/79455/7-moments-that-made-frozen-the-most-progressive-disney-movie-ever, "It's Not Just Frozen: Most Disney Movies are Pro-Gay," http://www.theatlantic.com/entertainment/archive/2014/04/its-not-just-frozen-disney-has-always-been-subtly-pro-gay/361060/

15. "Disney to pull Boy Scouts funding by 2015 over policy of banning Gay leaders," http://www.cnn.com/2014/02/28/us/disney-pulls-boy-scouts-funding

12: Discerning Culture

1. Augustine, "City of God," *The Nicene & Post Nicene Fathers: First Series*, ed. Phillip Schaff, trans. Marcus Dods (Peabody: Hendrickson, 2004), 5.13.

2. Ibid., 5.14.

3. "NASHVILLE SKYLINE: 'I Saw the Light' – A Country Music Beacon?" http://www.cmt.com/news/nashville-skyline/1491022/nashville-skyline-i-saw-the-light-a-country-music-beacon.jhtml

4. "J. S. Bach: Soli Deo Gloria - To the Glory of God Alone," http://www.christianity.com/church/church-history/church-history-for-kids/j-s-bach-soli-deo-gloria-to-the-glory-of-god-alone-11635057.html

5. see www.familyeconomics.com.

6. "Porn Stats," http://www.covenanteyes.com/pornstats/

7. "Walk On By (Leroy Van Dyke song)," http://en.wikipedia.org/wiki/Walk_On_By_%28Leroy_

Van_Dyke_song%29

8. "Same Trailer Different Park," http://en.wikipedia.org/wiki/Same_Trailer_Different_Park

9. "Composer Joseph Brooks' suicide a 'tragedy for everybody,' says his defense lawyer," http://www.nydailynews.com/news/crime/composer-joseph-brooks-suicide-tragedy-defense-lawyer-article-1.142591

10. "From Christian radio to a church near you," http://www.worldmag.com/2014/08/from_christian_radio_to_a_church_near_you

11. "Natalie Grant responds after leaving Grammys early; Mass wedding at award show criticized as 'political stunt' to push gay marriage agenda," http://www.christiantoday.com/article/mass.wedding.at.2014.grammys.criticized.as.political.stunt.to.push.gay.marriage.agenda.natalie.grant.responds.after.early.exit/35586.htm

General Index

Scripture Index